Win the *Whining* War
& Other Skirmishes

Win the *Whining* War & Other Skirmishes

A family peace plan

Cynthia Whitham, MSW

Illustrations by Barry Wetmore

PERSPECTIVE PUBLISHING

Los Angeles

Library of Congress Catalog Card Number 91-061008
ISBN 0-9622036-3-7

Published by Perspective Publishing, Inc., PO Box 41064, Los Angeles, CA 90041, 818-440-9635.

Additional copies of this book may be ordered by calling toll free 1-800-345-0096.

Publisher's Cataloging-in-Publication Data

Whitham, Cynthia
  Win the whining war & other skirmishes.
p. cm.
Includes index.
ISBN 0-9622036-3-7
    1. Discipline of children.   2. Parenting–United States.   3. Parent and child–United States.   I. Title
HQ770.4.W447 1991
649'.64–dc20   91-061008

Illustrations by Barry Wetmore
Back cover photo by Frank Bates
Printed in the United States of America
Second Printing: 1992

Acknowledgment

I am indebted to the UCLA Neuropsychiatric Institute and Hospital Parent Training Program which helps hundreds of families each year. The program was started in 1974 by Hans Miller, PhD and since 1983 has operated under the direction of Fred Frankel, PhD. The principles and techniques of the program are based on the research of Gerald Patterson, Rex Forehand, K. Daniel O'Leary, Fred Frankel and others. I especially wish to thank Fred Frankel for his continuing guidance and insight.

I was first introduced to the techniques of the program as a social work trainee and, upon graduation, found these indispensable to my work with teenage mothers and in my private practice. I returned to the Parent Training Program as a staff therapist in 1986, counseling parents and supervising child psychiatry fellows and social work interns. I saw these techniques work so well reducing conflict and stress in families with serious problems, that I wanted every family to have access to them.

In *Win the Whining War & Other Skirmishes* I have adapted the Parent Training Program's clinically effective concepts and methods. Admittedly, reading a parenting book is not the same as working for several weeks one-on-one with a therapist, but it is my hope that readers will find the material as useful as I have.

I thank the many client families who share with me their needs and concerns.

I thank Linda Goodman Pillsbury, my publisher, for her encouragement, enthusiasm, and patience throughout this project.

I thank my husband, Gearey McLeod for his support and love.

I am continually inspired by our children, Miranda and Kyle. Thank you both.

Contents

Introduction

Do whining, tantrums, talking back, bad language or sulking drive you crazy? You are not alone.

Our children interrupt us on the telephone, beg for junk toys in the market, dawdle getting dressed, test out lovely phrases like: "Why should I?" and "Who says?" They insist on ordering a cheeseburger and then decide it is too greasy, fat, thin, juicy, or burnt to eat, tease little sister until she screams, and never, ever pick up cast-off pajamas.

You may have chosen to be a parent, but you did not choose to give up your mental health in the process. I believe parents have a right to no-fuss mornings, tear-free bedtimes, low stress errand-running and time for themselves. *Win the Whining War & Other Skirmishes* gives you the tools to get a little more peace and a lot more cooperation from your kids. These tools have been used effectively by thousands of families at the UCLA

Neuropsychiatric Institute's Parent Training Program where I am staff therapist.

These tools will help you get more of the behaviors you like, less of the behaviors you dislike, and eliminate the behaviors you cannot tolerate. You will have an approach for almost every troublesome situation. You won't have to wonder, "Am I handling this correctly?"

Win the Whining War & Other Skirmishes can help your children, too. Nobody likes bratty, whiny, rude, and obnoxious behavior, and it feels horrible to BE bratty, whiny, rude and obnoxious. Your child will actually feel better when you consistently set firm, fair limits.

You are the key to changing your child. Because you matter so much to her, you have trememdous power to shape her behavior. Your attention, the way you respond to her, helps lock both desirable and undesirable behaviors in place.

Win the Whining War & Other Skirmishes gives you the tools to decrease your child's annoying habits by changing how you respond to them. When you know the tools well and apply them daily, your children's behavior will change. They will become more cooperative. Your mornings and bedtimes will run more smoothly. There will be less conflict. The entire family will feel better. *

You are the key to changing your child.
You can take control of your family.
You can WIN THE WHINING WAR & OTHER SKIRMISHES.

*If your child is under stress from big changes such as divorce, death in the family or moving, or if applying the techniques does not result in reducing problem behaviors, consider seeking counseling to help your family.

Step 1: Getting Started

In this section you will learn how to use
Win the Whining War & Other Skirmishes.
These three short chapters introduce the
major ideas and the simple framework you
will use to increase cooperation and
reduce conflict in your home.

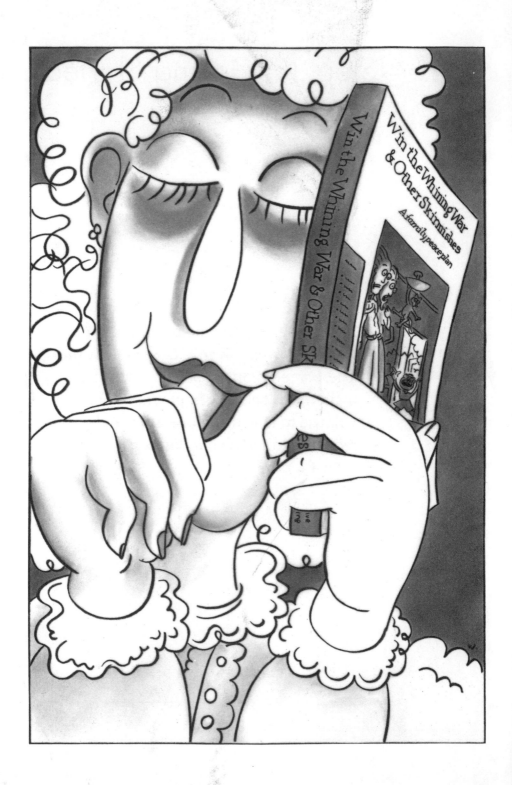

1
How to Use This Book

This is a step-by-step plan to increase cooperation and reduce conflict with children ages two to twelve. Each step builds on the one before.

In Step One you will be given a framework to apply to most problem situations. You will sort your children's behaviors into one of three categories: behaviors you like, behaviors you dislike and behaviors you find intolerable. For each type of behavior your child does, you will apply a different technique.

In Step Two you will learn how to give positive attention to increase the behaviors you like.

In Step Three you will learn to remove attention to decrease behaviors you dislike.

In Step Four you will learn invitations to cooperate, simple ways to get your child to start doing what you want.

In Step Five you will be taught firm, non-physical limit

setting tools for behaviors which are harmful or have become intolerable.

At the end of the book are the Battle Plans—brief, clear plans of action for the most common annoying behaviors, such as whining, tantrums, talking back, interrupting, sloppiness, using bad language, and fighting.

Read one step at a time. Think about each technique. Do the practice exercises. Try the technique with your child. When you have mastered that tool, go on to the next.

It may be tempting to flip to the limit setting part of the book or the Battle Plans, but I urge you not to. Each skill presented requires knowing the one before it. For example, in order to ignore, you must be able to praise. In order to set limits effectively you must be terrific at ignoring. You need to know all the tools to deal with your child's most challenging behaviors.

In my work with clients I find that those who practice the tools and use them habitually see changes in their children's behavior. The practice exercises will help you do the same. Certainly some of you will get a clear idea of the tools just by reading and may not have the energy or the time to write out an exercise. Others may find it effective to sit down with your spouse at the end of the day and talk about your child's behavior, using the practice as a guideline. Just remember: using the tools consistently is the key. If you don't see change occurring, go back and do each practice.

You may want to keep a spiral or looseleaf notebook and a pencil handy. Many parents find it useful to take notes, and the practice exercises involve keeping records of your child's behaviors.

The tools are simple, but they do require some effort and a little time. When you start using the techniques, consider giving yourself extra leeway. Start the bedtime ritual fifteen minutes before you usually do, get up twenty minutes earlier when you're trying to make the morning go smoother, or leave ten minutes earlier when you're applying the tools with that rowdy carpool. Once the behaviors improve, you may return to your previous schedule if you choose.

Every adult in the home should read *Win the Whining War & Other Skirmishes* and do the practice exercises. If you have a grandparent, sitter, or other adult to share the care, you will be more effective if you function as a team.

A note on gender–boys and girls whine, use bad language, hit, sulk, dawdle, and so forth. Most of the examples given can be applied to either gender. Rather than the cumbersome "his/her" or inaccurate "their," I've sprinkled the book with "he" and "she" and "his" and "her" and hope everybody feels included.

Keep a book on child development handy. Some respected authors include Arnold Gesell, Frances Ilg, T. Berry Brazelton, and Burton L. White. Read about your child's age. Read about the age before and the age after. Get a feel for what is "normal" emotionally, socially, intellectually, and physically. Each stage has its own difficult (as well as delightful) behaviors. You won't feel so alone if you know most parents are struggling with the same issues.

Read the book.
Apply the tools.
Increase the behaviors you like.
Decrease the behaviors you dislike.
Set firm, fair limits on the intolerable behaviors.
Inspire cooperation.
Celebrate the changes.
Win the Whining War & Other Skirmishes.

2
Changing Behavior: Attention is Powerful

We all need and want attention.

Imagine cooking a meal for your family. At the table there is silence. No "thank-you," no "Boy, this smells terrific!" Think how you feel putting extra time in at work, with no acknowledgment from the boss. Picture helping your neighbor and getting no word of gratitude. A day in which we and our efforts are ignored by our spouse, children, friends, neighbors, and co-workers is a bleak one.

Children need and want attention, too. Often they seem to have bottomless pits—no amount of attention is enough to satisfy. Your child does not suddenly get enough of your attention and then not want any more. Children's need of attention–adult attention—provides the key to increasing behaviors you like and decreasing behaviors you do not like.

Sometimes it seems as if a child would rather earn

NEGATIVE attention by getting into trouble, than POSITIVE attention for behaving well. It's as if she doesn't know how to do anything else. If your child seems to act up more than cooperate, it could be because she has discovered the quickest way to get your attention is by doing something you dislike.

In the busy lives we lead, we cannot always remember—or find the time—to give full attention to the story she wants to tell, the bug she has found on the grass, or the very bad joke she tells over and over. If our kids do chores without a squawk or play together without bickering, we keep quiet for fear of disturbing the peace. We wouldn't think of interrupting a child reading or playing solitaire to praise her. But if she is mean to her brother, bounces a ball off the ceiling, or uses bad language, we may quickly jump in with a lecture or other punishment. Every time we give more attention to the undesirable behaviors than we give to desirable ones, we are training our children to go for punishment (one form of attention) instead of going for praise (another form of attention).

We can shift the balance. Giving positive attention to behaviors you like encourages your child to do those behaviors more often. The more your child earns positive attention, the less tempting (and necessary) it is to earn punishment.

Let's take a behavior you like. You overhear your five-year-old child playing well with a friend. They take turns, are fair with each other, win and lose graciously. You can use your attention to increase this good behavior. You might say, "I was listening to you two play together. Joey, I liked the way you let Marc go first. And Marc, you were a very good sport when you lost the game—that's hard and you handled it well."

Your praising of Marc and Joey is giving positive attention. By giving positive attention, you are reinforcing the behavior. I like to picture it as tacking down the behavior with a little hammer and tiny tacks. Every time you praise a behavior you are tacking it in place more securely. Your child will do that behavior more often in order to get more of that positive attention from you.

Just the way you can increase the frequency of behaviors you like by giving your child positive attention, you can decrease the frequency of behaviors you dislike by removing your attention.

One day you hear Joey threaten Marc with "I won't be your best friend!" In the past you would rush to find out what was going on, perhaps telling Joey you were disappointed to hear him say that to Marc (who is indeed his best friend). You want very much to give a little lecture on friendship. In fact, you feel Joey's eyes turning to you for the expected look of disapproval. But this time you fight your impulse and leave the children alone. Soon they are playing well again, without your help! And now you praise them for working out their differences.

When you turn your attention away, you are removing the force that helps keep the behavior in place. By removing the payoff of attention, it is less likely your child will do that behavior again.

Practice:
Give a Little Attention

Try it out.
What is your child doing right how? A behavior you like?
(Since you are reading your child may be asleep!)

If your child is doing something you dislike, wait. As soon as he is doing a behavior you like, put the book down. Give him a little attention. Smile, pat his head or shoulder, show a little interest in the game, TV show, book, that he's absorbed in.

What happened? How did he react?

Did he seem to like it?
Was he surprised?
Did it feel good to you?
Did it feel a bit strange and unfamiliar?

Not so tricky, is it?
The more positive attention you give, the better things get.

IN SHORT

Children need and want attention from parents.

Parents can use the power of attention to change (shape) children's behaviors.

Giving positive attention (praising) increases behaviors you like and want more of.

Removing attention (ignoring) decreases behaviors you dislike and want less of.

3

Sorting Behaviors:
The First Step to Change

I promised you a framework you can apply to almost every problem situation. First divide your child's behaviors into three categories:

1. Behaviors you like and want to see more of.
2. Behaviors you dislike and want to see less of.
3. Behaviors you find intolerable and want stopped.

You do this sorting because the first step in facing a problem will be to ask yourself: Is this a behavior I like? (or is there any part of this behavior I like?) Is this a behavior I dislike? Is this a behavior I find intolerable? For each type you will learn different parenting tools.

Sorting behaviors allows you to stop, to see your child more positively, and to notice the little efforts and successes parents often take for granted.

Sorting behaviors makes you think about the difference between what you dislike and what you find intolerable. The difference may seem a small one, but the tools you use differ greatly.

For behaviors you like, you will learn to give positive attention, PRAISE. For behaviors you dislike you will learn to remove and refocus your attention, IGNORE. For intolerable behaviors, you will learn to SET FIRM LIMITS.

Behaviors you like and want more of don't have to be earth-shattering events like a straight-A report card or doing the dishes without being asked. They can be little things:

> a four-year-old cooperates while brushing teeth
> a twelve-year-old takes out the trash without complaining
> an eight-year-old starts (not finishes) her homework
> > without being reminded

Or:
> saying thank you when given something
> looking both ways before going into the street
> starting to get dressed (taking off pajamas)
> telling you about a school lesson
> complying with any request
> starting to comply with any request
> going to the market and not begging for a sweet
> reading
> playing quietly with brother or sister for five minutes
> turning off the TV voluntarily
> showing you a ladybug
> allowing you to talk on the telephone
> sharing a toy with a friend
> saying "excuse me" instead of interrupting
> telling the truth
> setting or clearing the table

putting on shoes by himself
waking up cheerfully
using an indoor voice (reasonably quiet)
letting parent brush teeth or hair
helping you in the house or yard
playing alone
doing part of his homework neatly or correctly
patting the baby gently
building with blocks instead of watching TV
using words when angry or frustrated instead of hitting
coming when called
hanging up jacket and backpack
giving you a hug or a kiss

Behaviors you dislike and want less of tend to be annoying, irritating, thorn-in-the-side types of actions. Not felonies, not misdemeanors, not even dangerous. You may feel they are INTOLERABLE, because you are sick and tired of their frequency or intensity, but because they do not involve harm to another, you include them in the DISLIKE category. These include:

dawdling
bickering with sister or brother
whining
complaining
talking back
using bad language
arguing
ignoring your request to do chores
not doing homework
being noisy in the car
name-calling
saying "I hate you"

teasing
interrupting
sulking
having a tantrum
tattling
refusing to get dressed
poking or shoving
leaving clothes on the floor

Intolerable behaviors are those involving harm or potential harm to people, pets, or property. This will not be a long list. Intolerable behaviors might include:

running into the street
hurting another child
spitting (not harmful—but intolerable anyway!)
biting a friend or sibling
playing with matches or a knife
breaking a family safety rule
being cruel or mean

Practice:
Sorting Behaviors

Take out your notebook and make three columns. Head them as follows:

Behaviors I like   Behaviors I dislike   Behaviors I find
& want more of   & want less of   intolerable & want
                                                   stopped

For each of these categories list four or five of your child's behaviors that come to mind.

The behaviors you choose need to fit this definition: an act you can see or hear. It's necessary to be very specific when you communicate with children. Using this definition will give you lots of practice being specific. For example:

> Rather than: be more polite
> List instead: says please and thank you at dinner

Your notebook entry might look something like this one:

Behaviors I like & want more of	Behaviors I dislike & want less of	Behaviors I find intolerable
getting dressed feeding the cats saying thank you sharing with friend helping with dishes	whining biting fingernails bickering with brother talking back calling me names	hitting little brother riding bike in street leaving house without my knowledge

Keep your notebook handy. A day or so after doing the practice, work a little more on your list. If only a couple of items come to mind, block out a part of a morning or an evening to observe your child and record more behaviors. Anytime a behavior comes to mind, add it to your list in the appropriate column.

If you don't have the time to make a list, begin to watch your child's actions. Decide: Is this a behavior I like and want more of? Dislike and want less of? Find intolerable?

IN SHORT

You start by looking at your children's behaviors — acts you can see or hear — and sorting them into three categories:

Behaviors you like.
Behaviors you dislike.
Behaviors you find intolerable.

Then after three of four days of practicing this sorting, you will be ready to learn the tools to:

Increase behaviors you like.
Decrease behaviors you dislike.
Stop the intolerable behaviors.

Step 2: Increasing Behaviors You Like

In this section you will learn to use the power of postive attention—praise and encouragement—to increase the behaviors your child does that you like and want more of. You will learn how and when to praise and how to make giving praise a daily habit. Although praise is a simple concept, it is not always easy to put it into daily use. The benefits to your family, however, are well worth the effort!

4

How to Praise:
Using the Elements

After a few days of identifying behaviors you like, you may have a pretty long list. You may find, like many of the parents I work with, that you are looking at your child in a new way, seeing what he has done rather than what he has not done, recognizing small successes and partial successes, appreciating him more.

How can you get more of these behaviors you like? Respond to him with positive attention. You will be rewarded with more of that terrific behavior. Giving positive attention may take several forms:

praising
encouraging
acknowledging
thanking
showing an interest in

For convenience, we will refer to all forms of positive attention as PRAISE.

I have to warn you. It does feel a bit embarrassing to say, "Great job, going poop in the potty!" or "Wow! You put on your left shoe so quickly!" or "I really like the way you are using your 'indoor' voice."

And don't be surprised if praising feels somewhat forced when you start. Correcting, complaining, and criticizing are familiar and all too easy to do. Encouraging, inviting, and (even) cheerleading seem a bit strange when connected to chores, responsibilities, and "things they should do anyway."

Trust me. When you start praising the behaviors you like, your child will do them more often. She will try out other desirable behaviors too, because the payoff (the positive attention) feels so good. Getting cooperation will be worth the momentary awkwardness and embarrassment you feel gleefully spouting, "I like how you're cooperating brushing your teeth!"

THE ELEMENTS

There is more to praising than just the words. Use the following elements to praise most effectively:

PRAISE THE ACT — not the child. You want to respond to the behavior, not the child as a person. So say, "Good job making your bed," not "Good boy."

TIMING — Praise as soon as possible: during or right after the act.

EYES — Make eye contact with your child. You want to be sure she hears you. Have her come to you or go to her.

BODY — Get on a level with your child. It is intimidating

to have a grown-up always towering above you (even a pleased grown-up). Crouching down to a little one makes him feel comfortable. Lean toward him. He'll feel your support and enthusiasm.

FACE — Smile if you feel like it! It communicates as much as your words.

TONE — Your tone should express the good feeling you have about what your child has done.

WORDS — Your message should be short, clear, and positive. Name the behavior so that your child knows exactly what he did that you like. Be genuine. Don't gush if you don't feel like it, but at least acknowledge that your child is doing what you like.

MAKE PRAISE MEANINGFUL — Think about the kind of positive attention your child would like best: verbal, non-verbal, quiet or loud, in front of others or whispered in her ear. Make it meaningful to her.

AVOID SARCASM — Your praise should not include any sour note, such as, "Good job—now if you'd only done that sooner..." or "Didn't I tell you that you could do it?" or any hint of sarcasm. These will spoil your effort at praising.

Example:

Ann: [feeds her dog without a reminder. Most of the time she must be nagged.]

Mom: [seeing her daughter do this] Ann, I see you are feeding Spike without being told. That's very responsible of you.

Although frustrated with having to nag Ann, Mom puts her feelings aside and is ready to praise. Here she:

1.   Takes time to go to her child.
2.   Names the behavior she likes—feeding the dog without a reminder.
3.   Tells why she likes the behavior—saying how responsible it is.

Ann will tend to feed her dog with fewer reminders because her mother responded to her with praise.

You may not always feel like praising, particularly if you have had to wait a long time for a behavior you like. In fact, your child may do something you like while you are feeling angry. When this occurs, simply give an acknowledgment. In our example, the mother could have said, "Thanks for feeding Spike." Giving positive attention can take several forms: encouraging, thanking, smiling at your child, showing an interest in what she's done that you like, or acknowledging the behavior.

SOME DO'S AND DON'T'S OF PRAISING

DO SAY:
   I love that picture. What gorgeous colors you've chosen.
DON'T SAY:
   You are the best artist in your class, better than anyone.
BECAUSE:
   You don't want your child's feeling successful to be at the
   expense of others. You don't want her to feel she has to be
   "the best" to be appreciated. She can't always be "the best,"
   and she may suffer a bitter disappointment when she finds
   herself less than perfect.

DO SAY:

You must be proud of yourself.

DON'T JUST SAY:

I'm proud of you.

BECAUSE:

Although your child wants to please you, it's more important that he feel pleased with himself. Telling your child, "You must feel really great about putting your shoes on all by yourself," let's him know it's fine to like himself—and that builds self-esteem.

DO SAY:

What a good job using the potty!

DON'T SAY:

What a good boy you are!

BECAUSE:

"Good boy" refers to his whole self. "Good job using the potty" (etc.) refers to the specific behavior. You don't want your child to feel that he can win or lose your love because of succeeding or failing at a behavior. Better for a child to feel "I'm in trouble because I poked my sister" than "I'm a bad boy." Again, this distinction is important for a child's self-esteem. We can't be sure that he's not thinking he's lost your love.

DO SAY:

What a great report card, Sarah.

DON'T SAY:

Great report card, Sarah, just like your big sister!

BECAUSE:

Comparing siblings fosters competition and resentment. Each child needs to feel she has earned her praise on her own merit.

DO BE GENUINE:

Most children will respond to any form of praise if it is genuinely given. It will be most effective, however, if you give some thought to making it meaningful to your child.

Praise can take many forms. Which will be meaningful to your child?

Praise can be:

verbal, a few words

non-verbal, like a thumbs-up sign

loud and big and gushy

quiet, whispered in the ear

a simple acknowledgment: "I see you've started on your homework."

an enthusiastic cheer: "Terrific job on your room!"

a reflection of the child's feeling: "You must feel great about that."

one parent telling the other: "Sam was a great helper today."

Practice:
Using the Elements of Praise

Start with your list of behaviors you like and want more of. When you see your child do one of these acts or something else you like, praise him. Then check yourself out. Are you using the elements? Refer to the following checklist until using the elements has become a habit:

Did I praise the behavior and not the child?

Did I have eye contact?

What did my body language say?
What was the expression on my face—pleasant?
How was my tone of voice—warm?
Did I name the behavior and keep my message brief?
Did I praise the behavior as soon as I saw it?
Did I praise her in a way she liked?

IN SHORT

For praise to be effective in increasing the behaviors you like and want more of, be sure to use the elements of praise.

Praise the behavior not the child.
Make eye contact.
Have your body on a level with your child, or give a hug or pat.
Have a smile or pleasant look.
Use a warm tone of voice.
Choose a short message that names the behavior you like.
Praise in a way that is meaningful to your child.
Praise IMMEDIATELY.

And of course, never sour praise with sarcasm or an "I told you so."

5
When to Praise

Most parents will praise a child when she finishes a task or complies immediately with a request to do a chore. If you are already doing that, wonderful. But don't stop there. Many parents have a tendency to praise only the completed task. That is the same as demanding perfection. Perfection is an unrealistic standard for children (and for adults!).

Try PRAISING THE PROCESS, praising your child throughout the task. When their ongoing effort is acknowledged and encouraged, children feel more appreciated and become more cooperative.

When you praise the process, you begin to see your child in a more positive light. Because you are looking for and finding small accomplishments, small steps in the right direction, you'll notice behaviors that you have been taking for granted. Your child, in turn, will feel the recognition and strive to cooperate more. If living with your child has been particularly stressful, you may actually feel yourself liking him more.

There are many opportunities to use praise with your child. When he:

STARTS to do a behavior you like
(begins to take off pajamas in the morning)

TRIES to do a behavior you like, even if unsuccessful
(puts a shoe on the wrong foot)

IS IN THE PROCESS OF doing a behavior you like
(working on homework)

COMPLIES with a request quickly
(starts toward bedroom when you've said it's bedtime)

SELF-STARTS — initiates
(picks up and puts away a game without a reminder)

PLAYS FAIRLY or SHARES WELL with another child
(is a good winner or good loser)

PLAYS by herself or himself
(reading, writing, drawing, building with blocks)

does THE OPPOSITE OF AN UNWANTED
BEHAVIOR
(uses a quieter indoor voice instead of yelling)

Praise in these situations and you will find an upward spiral of more and more positive interaction.

Practice:
Finding Opportunities to Praise Your Child

In your notebook write down the types of situations described above. For each type, list an example of a behavior your child does now. When each of these desirable behaviors occurs, praise your child.

If you have been focusing on your child's problems and misbehavior, this is an excellent opportunity to see the cooperation your child already gives you.

Your list of behaviors you like is a list that will change and expand. Different developmental stages bring different kinds of effort and accomplishment. You praise your three-year-old for putting on his shoes, your six-year-old for tying them, and your twelve-year-old for keeping his shoes off the couch! Each time you add a new behavior to this list let it remind you to praise. In this way you will ensure ongoing and increased cooperation.

Once again, if you do not have the time to sit and write out a list, do this practice in your head. Take note of his many efforts. And of course, praise them!

IN SHORT

Don't only praise perfection and completion of tasks.
Praise when your child:

> starts a behavior you like
> tries a behavior you like
> is in the process of a behavior you like
> complies quickly with a behavior you request
> initiates a behavior you like (self-starts)
> plays well with others
> plays by himself
> refrains from a behavior you dislike

Take notice of, appreciate, and PRAISE your child's success.
You have a terrific kid!

6
Making Praise a Habit

You know how to praise and when to praise. Now you must make it a daily habit to look for and identify your child's attempts at behaving well, and respond to them with positive attention.

The sooner praising is a habit—an unconscious response to your child's desirable behaviors—the sooner your child will begin that upward spiral of going for positive attention, and the sooner you will be relieved from that unwanted position of Chief Nag and Drill Instructor. I have never had a client for whom praise has not resulted in more cooperation.

Try it. Praise your child consistently for one week. Then keep on praising. You will be pleased with the results:

The behaviors you praise will increase.
Your child will feel better, more appreciated.
Your child will begin to cooperate in other areas.

You will feel better.
Family interactions will improve.
There will be less stress for all.

Remember: for praising to be effective, at first you must praise every time you see the behavior you like. Use the following Practice to help make praising a daily habit.

Practice: Making Praise a Habit

In your notebook make three columns. Head them as follows:

Time   Behavior I Liked   How I Praised

Keep the notebook handy. In one day record as many examples as you can of your efforts to praise your child. Fill half the page. More if you can. You cannot overdo this practice. A father of a nine-year-old might have entries like this:

Time	Behavior I Liked	How I Praised
7:00 a.m.	got out of bed when alarm rang	said,"Good morning, son, you're up nice and early."
7:30 a.m.	brushed teeth with no reminder	said, "Alan, good job remembering to do your teeth."
6:00 p.m.	started homework right after dinner without nagging	patted him on back & said, "Thanks for starting your homework."

Notice how the parent in the example praised:

He named the behaviors.
He used verbal and non-verbal attention.
He praised his child's work at the start.
He told his son how pleased he felt.

Review your examples. Are you using all the elements of praise? Are you praising the process and not just the finished product?

If possible, every adult in the home should do this practice. Each should keep his or her own list and at the end of the day compare them. Learn from each other. See what behaviors you missed or might not have thought to praise. Discuss what ways to praise were best received and most effective. The parent with the longest list deserves a prize—and praise of course.

IN SHORT

You must make praising a habit in order to get an upward spiral of cooperation from your child. Change will occur only when you are consistently responding with praise.

Practice is the key. In spite of feeling awkward and sounding silly—and you will feel awkward at first—praise anyway. Praise, praise, praise. As long as you are genuine, you can't overdo it.

Enjoy the results. Congratulate yourself.

Not only do you have a terrific kid, but you're a terrific parent!

Making a Big Task Manageable

You walk into the kitchen and see the dishes stacked up, food out on the counter, the cats meowing for dinner, a red glob of something on the floor, muddy handprints on the refrigerator and a wilting plant on the sill. You want to run.

When you tell a child to clean his room, get dressed, clear off his place at the table, and so forth, your child feels the same way. A task which may seem small to you can be overwhelming to your child. They want to run too. Yet their day is full of such demands.

There are two ways you can help make a large task more manageable for your child:

1. Break down the large task into smaller tasks.
2. Praise not only the start, but the ongoing effort.

A parent helps by suggesting, selecting, and naming the small parts of the big task. The child can picture the pieces in his mind and the whole job doesn't seem so overwhelming. After identifying each step of a job, the parent praises the start and the completion of each step.

All this may seem a lot of work, identifying each step and praising thoughout. It is at first. However, the payoff for you is great: your child will have the encouragement he needs to complete the job successfully.

Let's take the example of a three-year-old picking up his room. Let's break it down into smaller tasks:

Pick up the first toy—let's say a block.
Put the block in the toy box.
Put all the toy animals in the box.
Put the other toys in the box.
Put the books on the bookshelf.
Put the stuffed animals on the bed.
Put the dirty clothes in the laundry basket.
Put the scraps of paper in the waste basket.

By breaking down the big job into small, easily definable tiny jobs, the task "clean your room" or "pick up all your toys" will seem more approachable.

Is getting your child to dress herself an all-morning struggle? Maybe you are pleading, begging, then yelling and, finally, wrestling her into her clothes so you can get to work on time. Try praising after each of the small tasks and soon she will be dressing all by herself, in good spirits, and without your hovering over her!

Those small tasks might be:

takes off pajamas
puts pajamas in hamper

puts on underpants
puts on t-shirt
puts on pants
puts on one sock
puts on other sock
puts on one shoe
puts on other shoe
ties shoes

By the way, this is one of those times when you'll want to get your child up ten or fifteen minutes earlier for a week or two until things are running more smoothly. And have her select her clothes the night before!

This is a lot of effort, naming the next task, running in and out of the room, waiting patiently for your child to start to comply, praising each step in the right direction—but consider the payoff:

Soon your child is dressed.
There have been no tears and no nagging.
The child feels great.
The parent feels great.
Next time you can use less effort.
A few words of encouragement may soon be enough.

When you praise frequently you are no longer the nagging coach, you are a cheerleader. Who is more inspiring?

Practice:
Praising the Parts of a Task

Select a task that is a struggle for you to get your child to do.

A twelve-year-old must write a story or a research paper for school.

A five-year-old has left the kitchen table and floor a mess after a painting project.

A four-year-old's job is to empty small wastebaskets.

A nine-year-old needs to help fold his laundry and put it away.

A ten-year-old must clean out her hamster cage.

A six-year-old needs to write a thank you card to a grandparent.

A two-year-old must pick up crayons.

In your notebook, or in your mind, divide that task into as many small jobs as you can. Each one of these will provide an opportunity to praise your child.

You might start by reminding the child of the task but also saying something encouraging like, "It's time to start your homework. Why don't you work at the kitchen table so that if you have any questions I can help you?"

Praise the child as he starts the task. In this example you might give a few words of support, such as: "I'm glad you're starting early. That's a pretty big assignment."

As each piece is attempted or completed, comment on his effort. Be careful not to criticize. That can be very discouraging. Instead of correcting sloppy writing, look for a few words or lines on the page that are neat. Say something like: "I like the way your writing looks there, small and right on the line. I can read it very easily."

If you are busy—cooking dinner for instance—you might tell the child to call you after each part is done, say each line of math problems. That way, there is incentive for the child to complete each part. A child will want to finish a small task so he can call, "Dad! I'm done with that, come check my answers." You stir the pot one more time and go to him to check his work. You praise him for working quickly, tell him "Good job" for the correct answers, have him fix the errors, prompt him to do another line of problems and call you again. Back you go to check the chicken.

Make a big deal when your child finishes the whole job. One parent can praise the child to the other parent. A small child particularly loves to tell grandpa and grandma about "being a big helper" and a "good cooperator." In our example the dad can say, "Boy, you worked hard on your math tonight." You and your child will both feel good about the effort.

IN SHORT

Break a big job into smaller jobs whenever a task might be overwhelming to your child. Identify the smaller tasks for her as she works and praise her as she starts and completes each job. Soon the large task will be done, without tears and nagging. Next time the job will be easier.

The time you invest in praising now will pay off—and continue to pay off—in increased cooperation and more positive interaction with your child.

8
Finding More to Praise

Now you are familiar with the idea of praising your child when she complies with a request and attempts or completes a behavior you like. Hopefully it is becoming second nature for you and you feel less awkward. Your child is feeling more appreciated as you recognize her desirable behaviors.

Now I'd like you to think about praising behaviors which concern values and character, such as when your child:

MAKES A WISE CHOICE THAT YOU LIKE
(finishes homework before going out to play;
chooses to do art project instead of watching TV)

DISPLAYS A VALUE THAT YOU LIKE
(is generous with a brother or friend;
thinks of another's feelings)

REFRAINS FROM A PROBLEM BEHAVIOR
(uses words instead of hitting when angry)

EXHIBITS A MATURE BEHAVIOR
(starts book report early, not at the last minute;
ignores a bully's teasing)

FOLLOWS A FAMILY RULE IN SPITE OF
TEMPTATION
(asks for a treat rather than helping self;
rides bike inside boundaries though urged by friend to go
beyond)

EXHIBITS A QUALITY OF WORK OR PLAY THAT
YOU LIKE
(washes dishes without leaving them greasy;
does homework with neat handwriting and no smudge
marks)

When she does one of these, take her aside. Look her in the eye and tell her how pleased (or even proud) you are that she made that choice and that she should feel very good about it. You are making an investment in her repeating this type of good decision in the future.

Praise your child by specifically naming the behavior and naming the quality of that behavior which you like, as in this example:

Child: [puts newspapers on table before using glue to repair toy.]
Parent: Carla, thank you for putting on newspaper to protect the
            table. That was very careful of you.

Practice:
Finding More to Praise

Begin today to look for your child making wise choices, displaying values that you like, following a family rule despite temptation, and so on. Praise these subtle behaviors and watch them increase. Let your child know you see improvement and thank him!

IN SHORT

When you praise the behaviors you like and want more of, including:

> exhibiting mature behaviors
> following family rules
> displaying good values
> making wise choices, and
> substituting behaviors you like for problem behaviors,

you will ensure that your child will do these—and other positive behaviors—more often.

Step 3: Decreasing Behaviors You Dislike

In this section you will learn how ignoring (removing attention) decreases the behaviors your child does that you dislike and want less of. Like praise, ignoring is easy to understand, but parents find this the hardest tool to apply consistently. You will learn how to ignore, what to ignore, how to use the ignore/praise combination and ways to make ignoring easier. Then, watch those annoying behaviors decrease!

9

How to Ignore: Using the Elements

You have been using the power of attention to increase your child's desirable behaviors. In Chapter Two, I introduced the idea that removing attention will decrease behaviors you dislike and want less of. Removing attention is also called IGNORING.

"Ignoring?" you might wonder. "Ignoring tells my kid I don't care. He'll do anything he wants if I ignore it!"

Wait! Let's look at how people actually respond to being ignored:

You are standing on the curb waiting for your commuter bus. It's late. You check your watch. Time passes. No sign of a bus. Finally you decide to do something else. You walk, take a different bus, call a friend for a ride, find a cab.

Let's analyze this. Your behavior is standing and waiting for the bus. The bus is not coming. It is "ignoring" you. What do you do in response? You stop waiting and change your behavior. You walk.

Here's another example. You are at a party, talking with someone, telling him a story about a terribly cute thing your child did. Your companion begins to break eye contact with you, slightly turns away, smiles and nods to others. He is ignoring your story telling.

Your response? You cut short your tale, stop talking or perhaps ask him a question to engage him again. He ignores you and you stop your behavior.

This is exactly how ignoring works with children. Because children want and need our attention so very much, removing attention has great power to change their behavior.

I am not saying "ignore your child." I am saying "ignore your child's behavior." The difference is important. You are not punishing your child with silence. You are not even sulking or fuming to show disapproval. You are giving the message: "This is a behavior I do not like. You are going to get no payoff, no attention from me, as long as it continues."

When followed by praising the behavior you want in its place, ignoring is a powerful form of limit setting. In fact, the key to ignoring is the praising afterward, as soon as you see a behavior you like. By ignoring, you reduce the behavior you dislike, and by praising, you show your child the behavior you want instead.

Maybe you have already discovered the power of ignoring, with behaviors such as tantrums and whining. In great frustration, parents sometimes turn away when their child has a full blown tantrum. To their surprise, they find the child gives up—runs out of juice—and quiets. Or parents might respond to whining by saying, "I'm not going to listen to you until you talk to me in a normal voice." In effect, they are announcing to their child they will ignore her until she stops the whining. If they successfully ignore the whining and then praise the child's use of her "big girl" voice, they are well on the way to eliminating the behavior.

Don't take my word for it. Read the rest of this chapter. Try ignoring those behaviors you dislike and want less of. If you use ignore/praise consistently you will be thrilled with the results.

Removing attention from a behavior may take several forms. You may:

turn away
change the subject
repeat what you just said
focus on something else
break eye contact
announce you are not going to hear or see a behavior and
    then do not pay any attention to it

We will refer to all forms of removing attention as ignoring.

THE ELEMENTS

Ignoring involves turning your face and body from your child while she is doing the behavior you dislike. At the same time you hide your feelings of anger and frustration. You are aware of her, waiting for a behavior you like, but you focus on something else. You are prepared to praise her as soon as she switches from an irritating behavior to one that's desirable.

To ignore effectively use these elements:

EYES — Make no eye contact with your child. Show him you are not attending to his behavior.

BODY — Turn away to show you are not interested in his behavior (even if it is not true).

FACE — Neutral, detached expression. No sign of anger (even if you are angry).

MESSAGE — NONE! No words, no nonverbal cues. No sighs of exasperation.

EMOTION — NONE! Not angry, not fed up, not anything! Focus on the second hand of your watch, music on the radio, a speck of dust on your shirt.

TIMING — Ignore immediately, as soon as a behavior you dislike begins.

BE READY TO PRAISE as soon as your child stops the behavior you dislike and starts a behavior you do like. Ignoring only works when followed by praise. By ignoring, you decrease what you dislike and by praising you increase the desirable behavior you want in its place.

Be prepared: when you start to ignore, your child will wonder where all the attention (complaining, correcting, criticizing, and so forth) went. He will do more of the behavior to try to get that attention you are refusing to give. It's as if he is saying, "Maybe you can't hear me. I'll scream a little louder! I'll kick a little harder! Can you hear me NOW?" This is when you must dig in your heels and continue to ignore.

Let's look at the example of a father using ignoring in the market. At the check-out stand, his three-year-old child Olga sees a display of gum.

Olga: I want gum, daddy.
Father: No, Olga, I'm sorry. It's bad for your teeth.
Olga: [louder] I want gum. I want gum.
Father: I'm sorry, no.
Olga: [crying] I want gum. Give me gum!

Olga's father now turns away, and starts putting groceries

from the cart onto the counter. Olga falls onto her knees and clutches her father's pant leg. He takes a couple deep breaths and calmly picks up a magazine to read. Olga's crying increases for several minutes, and then, as her father puts the magazine back on the rack, chats with the checker and pays his bill, her crying starts to subside. He waits for a behavior he likes. Eventually Olga gets to her feet.

Father: Would you like to help push the cart?
Olga: [still pouting, sniffling a bit, nods yes]
Father: Thank you, it's very full and heavy.

This father ignores correctly:

1. He turns away, gives no attention.
2. He focuses on other things and people.
3. He takes a couple of deep breaths to stay calm.
4. He attends to Olga when she finally quiets.

If Olga's father uses the ignore/praise combination every time she demands gum in the market, she will eventually cease creating a scene and begin to accept "no."

I like to think of ignoring as waiting for a behavior you like. You might think, "Wait? Who has the time—or patience—to wait?" (I'll talk more about this in Chapter 11). I urge you to take the time to ignore. When you expect a tantrum (because your child daily resists brushing his teeth, for instance), try to allot yourself extra time so that you can more calmly wait for a behavior to praise. You must be able to outlast your child. Your temptation will be to give in, but if you do, you will tack that undesirable behavior into place by the attention that you give it. It will be even harder after that to turn the behavior around.

Certainly, once you are using the ignore/praise combination consistently, the time you need to wait for the behavior to subside will be shorter. You will have built up some credibility. Your child will know that when you ignore, you mean business, and you will not reward her with attention. The incidents will be fewer, shorter and easier.

ANNOUNCING YOU WILL IGNORE

It can help to announce to your child that you will ignore her behavior, provided you follow through with exactly what you say. Above, when Olga began to cry, her father could have said, "Olga, I am not going to listen to you until you are quiet." He then would have ignored all her words and actions until she had complied.

Practice:
Using the Elements of Ignore

Start with your list of behaviors you dislike and want less of from the Chapter Three practice. When you see your child do one of these—bickering with her sister, arguing back, biting fingernails, moping—try ignoring her. Then check yourself out. Are you using the elements? Refer to the following list as a reminder until using the elements has become a habit:

> Did I look away from my child? Have no eye contact?
> Was my body turned away, so I looked as if I were not
>   paying attention?
> The look on my face—was it neutral, blank?
> Was I silent? No verbal or nonverbal message? No sighs?
> Did I appear emotionless, detached, calm?
> Did I start ignoring right after the behavior I disliked
>   started or after I announced I would ignore it?
> Did I praise when my child stopped the behavior or
>   started a behavior I liked?

IN SHORT

For ignoring to be effective in decreasing the behaviors you dislike and want less of, be sure to use the elements of ignore:

    make no eye contact
    turn away from your child
    focus on something else (your watch, your breathing,
        counting to ten, a book)
    have a neutral, blank face
    make no sound, give no verbal or nonverbal message
    stay calm, emotionally detached
    ignore IMMEDIATELY

    and PRAISE when the behavior stops or one you like starts.

10
When to Ignore

Whenever your child does a behavior you dislike and want less of, ignore that behavior. Keep ignoring until he does a behavior you like, then give praise. You may use ignoring with all of the behaviors from your list of behaviors you dislike and want less of from Chapter Three. Sometimes it is easier to start by ignoring only one behavior at a time.

Remember that when you start to ignore a behavior it will increase for a short time before it starts to decrease, but if you persevere and keep on ignoring, the behavior will decrease. By praising the opposite of the undesirable behavior, you will teach your child what behavior you want in its place. The following practice will help you identify when to use the ignore/praise combination.

Practice:
Using the Ignore/Praise Combination

1. Take out your list of behaviors you dislike and want less of.

2. For each behavior you dislike, jot beside it the behavior you want in its place.

Behavior I Dislike	Behavior I Want Instead
whining	using a "big boy" voice
hitting mom	saying, "I'm mad" to express anger
complaining in the car	being patient
tantrums	accepting "no" from parent
sulking	telling the problem to parent

3. Pick one behavior you want to decrease, and try ignoring that target behavior whenever that behavior occurs.

4. As soon as a behavior you like occurs, praise.

5. Any time the behavior you want in place of the target behavior occurs, praise.

You can prove the effectiveness of the ignore/praise combination. Keep a record for a week. Note every time the target behavior occurs. You will see the behavior decreasing.

Keep up the good work. This is the hardest tool in the book. For extra help see Chapter Eleven.

IN SHORT

To decrease behaviors you dislike:

1. Identify a behavior you dislike and want less of and IGNORE it.
2. Decide what behavior you want instead and PRAISE it.
3. Be prepared to see a slight increase in the behavior but KEEP IGNORING.
4. Count every time the target behavior occurs.
5. Watch the target behavior decrease.
6. Congratulate yourself—you're doing a great job!

11
When Ignoring Seems Impossible

Most parents have difficulty ignoring some behaviors at least some of the time.

You are driving along the freeway and your kids are whining about how bored they are, how long it's taking, how one is taking up all the room...you get the picture.

You are on the telephone, trying to have a conversation with a friend. Your two-year-old child pulls at you, wanting to talk himself, or wanting you off the phone.

It's after work. You are cooking and ask for some help washing the vegetables. Your seven-year-old child protests, "Why do I have to do everything?"

Many of the behaviors we want to decrease are so annoying that parents can barely keep from losing their temper. "How can I ignore," parents ask me, "It is impossible to do nothing!" But the secret to ignoring is not to do nothing but to do something else, to focus on something other than your child's annoying behavior.

One reason ignoring is hard is that many of us were raised by mothers and fathers who were great at criticizing, correcting, and complaining. We repeat those old parenting styles without thinking. We are embarrassed at hearing ourselves being sarcastic or perfectionist with our little ones. But we learned these ways before we could speak or reason. Unless we consciously replace these habits with new tools, we will return to them. And our children will use the old ways with their children!

The problem with all that correcting, criticizing, and complaining (verbal punishment) is that it is giving attention. The way to decrease behaviors is to remove attention.

Some parents worry that ignoring a behavior is giving your child permission to do that behavior. It is not. It gives the child the message, "I do not like that behavior and you will get no attention for it."

Some clients tell me that in a frustrating moment with their child they forget to try ignoring. One couple found a way to help each other remember. When their son does a behavior they don't like and one parent starts to respond, the other will say, "Oh, honey, Mrs. Doolittle called." Not only does this signal the other to ignore, but it allows him to leave the room if he needs to, announcing, "Thanks, I'll call her right now."

I also hear from parents that they start to ignore a behavior but give up too soon, worn down by their child's persistence. This is understandable, for when you start to ignore a behavior, say name-calling, your child will do it more frequently for a bit, to try to get back your attention.

This is the most crucial time to KEEP IGNORING. You must outlast your child. Every time you give in or yell, you are tacking that behavior in place. I know ignoring is not easy, but it is worth the effort.

TRUST ME!!! When you have consistently ignored a target behavior and religiously followed through with praise when your child finally does a behavior you like—you will have success. Ignoring may be the hardest tool you will have to learn, but it has helped thousands of families and can help you too.

So. When you find that:

> You feel too stressful or angry to ignore a behavior
> You can't remember to ignore a particular behavior
> You start out ignoring a behavior but end up yelling or
>   punishing or even giving in

that's when you need a Plan of Action to help you focus your attention away from your child's behavior and to remind you to praise.

Practice:
Ignoring Action Plan

Review your list of behaviors you dislike and want less of.
Select one target behavior which you want to stop.

In your notebook make a plan of action for ignoring that target behavior by answering the following questions:

1. What behavior do I dislike and want less of?
2. What behavior do I want in its place?
3. Where does the behavior I dislike occur?
4. When does it occur?
5. What else is happening at the time?
6. When the behavior occurs, what will I do? (include eyes, body, emotions)
7. What will I focus on, instead of the behavior?
8. What little pep talk can I give myself?

9. What will I do when he stops the behavior I dislike or starts a behavior I like?
10. What will I do if he does not stop the behavior?

Example:

Six-year-old Tina comes into the kitchen where her mother Maggie is finishing cooking dinner for the two of them. Maggie asks Tina to set the table. Tina yells at her mother, "You treat me like Cinderella!" Maggie is furious. Her friends' children do far more chores than Tina and she thinks it's about time that Tina start helping a little. But Maggie, who is a single mother, hates confrontations with Tina, particularly around dinnertime. She would like dinner to be a relaxed and chatty time for the two of them. She avoids the situation by saying, "Well, tonight you don't have to set the table. But starting tomorrow setting the table will be your job, just like cooking is my job."

Riding to work the next day Maggie decides, "I have a right to ask Tina to set the table. Setting the table is a reasonable request for a six-year-old, or even a four-year-old!" She's dreading the confrontation that evening. She knows Tina will be angry, will respond with arguing and complaining or a full blown tantrum. On her lunch break she prepares an Action Plan like this one:

1. What is the target behavior that I dislike and want less of?
   Complaining, whining, screaming, stomping out of the room.

2. What behavior do I want in its place?
   Setting the table or at least discussing it with me calmly.

3. Where does the tantrum occur?
   In the kitchen.

4. When does it occur?
   About 6 o'clock. Right before dinner.

5. What else is happening at the time?
   I am cooking. We are hungry, tired, and cranky. She is
   watching TV which she loves to do. She hates to be
   interrupted. I even let her do her homework after TV
   and supper because I hate the arguing.

6. When the behavior occurs, what will I do? (include
   eyes, body, emotions)
   First I will tell Tina calmly, but firmly, "When you
   have set the table, then I will serve dinner."
   Next, when the protests start, I will slowly look away,
   turn away, and try to keep my breathing relaxed.

7. What will I focus on instead of the tantrum?
   I will turn to my cooking, stir the vegetables, check
   the pasta, put some bread into the oven. There are lots
   of things I have to do anyway, so it will be easy to
   appear that I'm not listening, even if I am.

8. What pep talk can I give myself?
   If I ignore this, it will stop. I can do it. She's a little
   girl. I am the grown-up here. I have a right to have
   some help and children need to do chores. If I never
   give her responsibilities, she will become a spoiled
   monster.

9. What will I do when she stops the behavior I dislike
   or starts a behavior I like?

When she has stopped complaining, fussing, arguing and carrying on, I will turn my attention to her. Maybe I'll ask her a non-controversial question or offer her a choice. I might say, "Would you like milk or juice to drink?" That will break the ice and let her know I'm not holding any grudge. Maybe I'll give her a little understanding by saying, "You must be as hungry and tired as I am!" If she starts to set the table, I will say, "Thanks, Tina, I do appreciate your help."

10. What will I do if she does not stop the behavior I dislike?
    She might not stop! She might cry herslf to sleep. I think that if I appear firm she will eventually set our places at the table, but I have to be prepared that she may not give in. Maybe I can think of a face-saving compromise I could offer her. Perhaps when dinner is all ready I could say, "I'm done with my job, I will help you." I could hand her the forks at the same time. I'm pretty sure she would take them and start to set the table.

This Action Plan helps Maggie prepare for the conflict with Tina she knows will come. By having a plan, she avoids that horrible moment parents feel of "Help! What should I do?"

The Action Plan helps Maggie think about Tina's behaviors: Is there any part of this behavior that I like? What behavior do I want in its place? What part of this behavior do I dislike? It reminds her to ignore what she doesn't like and wait to praise behaviors she does like.

By planning what Maggie will focus on, she will be more likely to remember to ignore and she will be able to ignore when the situation gets tense. She can practice in her mind, or even better, actually on her feet, before the confrontation with Tina.

A pep talk can be as simple as, "Hang in there. You can do it!" But it can also be a few words that help you commit yourself. Maggie is torn. She wants Tina to set the table, yet she wants peace. As long as she is vacillating back and forth, Tina will sense her ambivalence and will not cooperate. In her pep talk Maggie reminds herself she is the parent. She has a right to a little help with setting the table. More importantly, Tina must learn that she has responsibilities, that in every family—especially small, single parent families—all the members must pull their weight. It is the parents' job to give this invaluable lesson to their child.

Maggie must find the strength to ignore every time Tina throws a tantrum for quite a while. Because in the past, she has given in to avoid a fight, Maggie has taught Tina that all she has to do is fuss enough and she'll get what she wants. Maggie must undo the effects of that habit!

Ignoring a particularly irritating behavior—sulking, using bad language, arguing—can be stressful and challenging. When you identify a new target, use the Action Plan to build your strength to ignore. By deciding exactly what you will ignore and how you will ignore it, what you will do and what you will say, even what you will think—you help yourself successfully ignore and decrease the unwanted behavior.

Ignoring eventually will become second nature, an effective weapon in your arsenal.

IN SHORT

Ignoring is a powerful way to reduce unwanted behaviors, but it is not easy. It takes practice. To help you ignore a particularly annoying behavior, prepare yourself by making an **Action Plan**. Answer the following questions:

' 1. What behavior do I want less of?
2. What behavior do I want in its place?
3. Where does this occur?
4. When does it occur?
5. What else is happening at the time?
6. When the behavior occurs, what will I do? (include eyes, body, emotions)
7. What will I focus on instead of the behavior?
8. What pep talk can I give myself?
9. And when the behavior I dislike stops and a behavior I like starts—how will I give praise to encourage more of the behavior I like?
10. What will I do if my child will not stop?

12
Making Ignoring a Habit

You know how to ignore and when to ignore. You have an Action Plan to help you ignore when it is difficult. Now you must make ignoring a habit—a knee jerk response to seeing behaviors you dislike. Why? Ignoring some of the time does not work. You must ignore every time for the behavior you dislike to decrease.

Sheila, the mother of a six-year-old boy listed in her "behaviors I dislike" column "calls me to come for every little thing." Her habit of dropping what she was doing and running to her child's side began when he was an infant. Appropriately, she responded to his cries and calls, but now he was old enough to come to her. Sheila felt like his personal maid and resented it.

She decided to use the ignore/praise combination. In a family meeting she told her son that if he seriously needed her, if he were hurt or scared for instance, she would go to him when he called, but he was old enough to come to her if he wanted to show her something. She announced that from then on when he called to her she would not come, but would let him know where she was by calling back "in the kitchen" or "in the bedroom." Then he could find her.

Sheila started off enthusiastically, but found it hard to use ignore/praise consistently. Sometimes she forgot and went to him. Sometimes she got mad and shouted, "Don't call, come here!" Because she was not consistent, his calling actually increased! I asked her to do the "making ignoring a habit" practice (below).

Recording his behavior and her response helped. Soon Sheila could catch herself if she started to go to him. When he called her, she called back "in the laundry" or wherever. She knew that if he really needed her he would let her know. Sometimes he called, "Never mind" and other times he came running to her. When he did, she would praise him with, "Thanks for finding me." Then she'd give whatever help or attention he needed.

Sheila had to break her own habit in order to break his habit. She had to stick to her ignore/praise plan.

Use the practice "making ignoring a habit" to address behaviors you dislike and want to decrease.

Practice:
Making Ignoring a Habit

In your notebook make four columns. Head them as follows:

Behavior I Disliked   How I Ignored   What I Praised   How I Praised

Keep the notebook handy. In one day, record as many examples as you can of your efforts to ignore your child's behaviors. Fill half the page. Fill the whole page. The more you practice ignoring the more powerful a tool it will become.

The parent of a nine year-old might have entries like this:

Behavior I Disliked	How I Ignored	What I Praised	How I Praised
sulking	listened to radio	she asked to talk to me	sat with her & listened to her; tried to understand
talked back to me when I said she couldn't go out until she helped with dishes	made a phone call, turned away	she apologized to me, started helping me do dishes	"thank you for apologizing," talked with her, we did dishes together
teased brother about poor test mark in math	gave brother some comfort	she told her brother that one bad test won't hurt	gave her a hug, "I appreciate how you tried to cheer him up"

Review your examples.

Are you using the elements? (See Chapter Nine.)

Are you looking for—waiting for— a behavior to praise?

Notice how the parent in the example used ignore/praise:

1. She focused on the radio or the telephone.
2. She turned her attention to someone else.
3. When the child did a behavior the parent liked, the parent welcomed her back with praise (verbal, non-verbal, offer of help, empathy, thanks).

Attention from any family member will help keep the target behavior occurring! Teach adults and other children the power of ignoring. Ask for their help with a particularly stubborn behavior.

IN SHORT

The ignore/praise combination is effective when you use it consistently, every day, with behaviors you want to decrease.

Don't give up. Pick a behavior you dislike and ignore it. Praise the behavior you want in its place and give yourself lots of pep talk. It will work wonders for reducing those annoying behaviors and increasing the terrific ones.

13

Inspiring Cooperation with Two or More Children

Believe it or not, two children or a group of children can be more manageable than one child. (I didn't say quieter, I said more manageable.) You simply apply the tools of praising and ignore/praise to the group of children as you would to one child. Think how often we have more than one child in our company:

> you have two or more children
> cousins or friends come visiting
> carpools to school, lessons, temple or church
> birthday parties
> cooperative child care/babysitting for friends
> potlucks
> outings to beach or movies
> community, social, or political events
> spending time in your child's classroom

These times can run more smoothly by remembering these simple rules:

1. When you see one child do a behavior you like—PRAISE HIM.

2. If a child does a behavior you don't like—but don't quite find intolerable—IGNORE THE BEHAVIOR.

3. Look for—and find—a child who is doing what you want (cooperating) and then,

4. PRAISE THE COOPERATING CHILD, while continuing to ignore the misbehavior of the other child.

5. Wait and PRAISE as soon as the uncooperative child complies.

Let's look at an example. Mrs. Medina is taking her children, Rosa and Sam, and their friends, Doris and Peter, to a movie. The behaviors she wants from the children are:

keeping their hands to themselves
wearing seat belts in the car
using indoor voices in the car and movie theater
holding hands crossing the street

Behaviors she does not want are:

hitting
standing up in the car
bickering or yelling
running in the street

Mrs. Medina uses ignoring when:

> Rosa says, "I hate seatbelts."
> Peter's voice starts to gets louder.
> Sam runs ahead a bit on the walk.
> Doris says, "I don't want to sit next to my brother; he smells."
> The boys start poking each other a bit.

Mrs. Medina looks for and finds the child who is doing what she likes and praises the cooperating child. She uses such phrases as:

> "Great job, boys, putting on your seat belts so quickly."
> "Thank you, Sam, you're using a nice, quiet indoor voice."
> "Rosa, thanks for taking Doris' hand. I didn't even have to remind you!"
> "I like how you girls are keeping your hands to yourself."

Rather than play into a downward spiral of misbehavior, Mrs. Medina shapes the children's behavior using the ignore/praise combination. She rewards the cooperative child with praise and removes the expected payoff of punishment. Pretty soon the girls are putting on their seatbelts, Peter's lowered his voice, the boys aren't poking, and Sam and Peter are holding hands on the sidewalk.

Please note that although the mother is praising the other children's behavior, she is not actually comparing them or putting down any of the children. The purpose is to invite cooperation, not belittle them in any way.

Wrong: Doris and Rosa, can't you buckle your seat belts like the boys?

Right: Sam and Peter, thanks for putting on your seat belts so fast!

This inspiring one child by praising the good example of another may be applied to many situations, including:

One child hasn't touched his peas, while his sister has
    eaten some:
"Good job eating those peas, Maggie."

One child is dawdling getting dressed, while the other is
    all dressed:
"I see you have on your shoes, Matt. Great!"

One child has not cleaned his part of the room, while his
    brother has:
"Nick, your side of the room looks terrific. Thanks."

One child is yelling, while another is using a voice you
    can tolerate:
"Mario, thanks for using a quiet voice!"

One child will not share his markers with the group, while
    another offers hers.
"Sachi, how nice of you to share your markers!

In situations like these, praise so that the other child can hear. Then wait—ignoring non-compliance—for the other child or children to do a behavior you like. When she does, GIVE POSITIVE ATTENTION, PRAISE.

Practice:
Inspiring Cooperation with Two or More Children

Pick a behavior you dislike and want less of that involves more than one child. Decide what is the opposite of that behavior.

The next time you get the behavior you dislike—IGNORE IT. Watch for the other child to give you the behavior you want. Then praise him for the behavior you like.

Example:

> When you call the children for dinner, one usually dawdles or protests. Praise the child who comes toward you, or who calls "Coming," with a simple "Thank you for coming so quickly." Do not show attention to the other child. She will soon follow the example of the praised child, because she wants the attention too.

In your notebook make three columns labeled as follows:

Behavior I Wanted   How I Praised   What Happened
from one child   the other child   Next

Each time you attempt to shape a child's behavior by praising another child's behavior, add it to your list as in this example:

Behavior I Wanted from Leah	How I Praised Allison	What Happened Next
stop stepping in mud puddles	said, "Thanks for walking around the mud puddles."	Leah said, "Mom, see, I'm jumping over the puddles!"

This tool will become one of your most valuable. You will be focused on the good behaviors, rather than on the undesirable ones. You will handle situations which have been tense in the past more calmly. Keep practicing, until you have made this IGNORING ONE, PRAISING ANOTHER second nature.

IN SHORT

In a group of two or more, praise the behaviors you like of one child to get another child to stop doing behavior you dislike. Be sure to praise when you get cooperation!

Remember never to compare—

Wrong: See Elliot, what a good job Ben is doing?
Right: Ben, that's a great job you're doing!

Step 4: Inspiring Cooperation

In this section I introduce four invitations to cooperate. These techniques encourage cooperation and lower confrontation when you want your child to do a chore or a task. Giving your child a Choice, using an Announcement, and making a When/Then Deal are three simple tools which are great alternatives to nagging—and work much better.

The Better Behavior Chart (BBC) is a several week program which addresses particularly problematic times of day (before school or bedtime) and generates greater cooperation throughout the entire day.

The more cooperation you can inspire, the less you will have to command with sterner measures (Step Five).

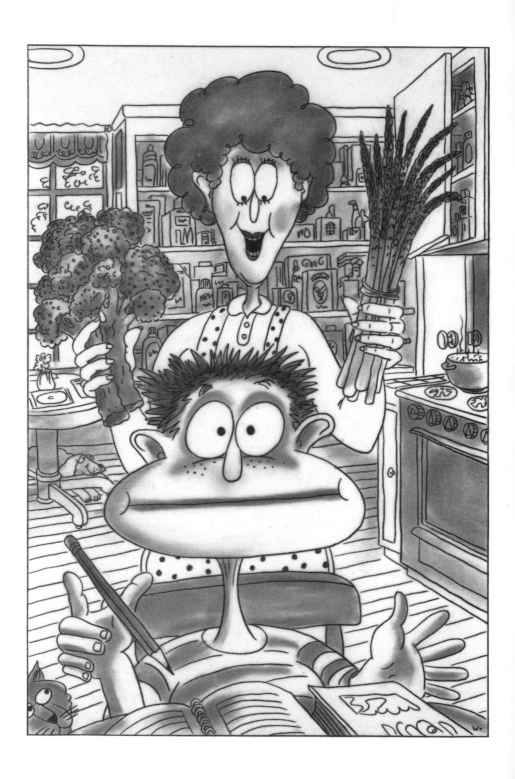

14
Offering a Choice

A CHOICE is the offer of two or more options—one of which your child must pick. Offering a choice, rather than making a demand, keeps communication open. Kids have to comply with demands all the time. A choice doesn't feel so inflexible. Why not give them a little control in their daily lives by giving them a few more options? Here are some examples:

You want your child to put on pajamas for bed.
"Which pajamas do you choose, pink or striped?"
UNDERSTANDING: it's time to put on pajamas.

You want your child to empty trash baskets.
"Will you empty the trash—now or after breakfast?"
UNDERSTANDING: she must empty the trash this
    morning.

You want your child to put on shoes for school.
"Do you want to put on your shoes yourself or would you
    like me to help?"
UNDERSTANDING: he needs to put on his shoes.

Most children will feel better about complying with a request if they have some say in the matter. When your child makes his choice, praise him with a simple "thank you" or "good choice."

Your child may suggest a third possibility. If it is workable, go with it. If it is not a good alternative, present your offer again.

Your child may challenge you by responding, "I don't want to do either." If he does, you should simply repeat the offer. If he still does not choose, you may need to say, "Then I will choose for you." Stay calm and neutral and give praise when you finally come to agreement. For example:

Dad: It's pretty cold tonight. Do you want to wear your sweater
        or your jacket?
Matt: Neither.
Dad: Your sweater or your jacket?
Matt: I don't want to wear anything. I'm not cold.
Dad: If you can't choose, I will choose for you.
Matt: Okay, okay. How about my sweatshirt?
Dad: Your sweatshirt will be fine, Matt. Thank you.

Because it is a particularly cold night, the father in this example offers his child the choice of wearing a sweater or a jacket. The understanding is "You will dress warmly tonight." When he gives the choice Matt resists. Matt's dad then:

1.   Repeats the offer.
2.   Tells child he will choose for him.
3.   Accepts a workable third option suggested by his son.

If your child of any age protests or throws a tantrum, ignore until he quiets and present the choice again. If this does not result in cooperation, use a limit setting tool from Step Five.

Practice:
Offering Choices

Identify a behavior you want from your child. Rather than telling her what to do (with a command), offer him a choice. Remember that underlying the offer is the understanding that your child must choose one or the other.

If your child selects another option that is acceptable to you, fine. If she refuses to choose, tell her you will choose for her, and do so.

Stay calm. Repeat the offer if she attempts to divert you with sarcasm, comments, or arguments.

Praise when she chooses and when she does the behavior.

IN SHORT

When you want your child to do a task, offer him a choice of two options. When he chooses, give praise. If he presents a third option, accept it if it is workable.

Underlying the offer of a choice is the understanding that the child must choose to cooperate. Be sure to praise when he chooses and does the task.

15
Announcements

An ANNOUNCEMENT is a statement that lets your child know that a command is coming and soon she will have to stop what she is doing and do something else.

No one likes to be interrupted. Children at play do not like being told, "Stop playing and come in for supper." However, making an announcement will help your child prepare for the transition. Relieved to have a little more time to play, he will more easily accept the reminder when it comes a few minutes later.

Examples:

Dad: Three more times down the slide and we'll have to go home.
Three slides later: David, it's time to go now.

Mom: Susie, in five minutes you will need to pack your
     backpack for school.
Five minutes later: Susie, it's time to pack for school.

If your child says, "Okay, Mom." That's great. "Okay" is an agreement. Sure, their eyes are glued to the TV, video screen, game board—and the agreement might not hold up in a court of law—but welcome it anyway. Say, "Thank you."

Give announcements when you need to interrupt your children. You may get resistance and protests at times, but you are more likely to get cooperation if you prepare them than if you use a direct command.

Practice:
Making Announcements

Identify a behavior you want from your child.

Rather than waiting until the moment you need the behavior done, give your child an announcement five, ten, or at the most fifteen minutes earlier. For a child under five, say "Three more times... "

When the time is up, follow through with a command.

Example:

   You want Sally to come in from play because it is time
      for bath.
   You go to the doorway and call, "Sally, in fifteen minutes
      it will be time for your bath."
   Fifteen minutes later: "Sally, time for bath now."

Your child's room is a mess and he is watching television.
You say, "Michael, in ten minutes it will be time to turn
    off the TV and clean your room."
Ten minutes later: "Time to clean your room now,
    Michael."

You want your children to do their chores, but they are
    playing cards.
You announce, "When you've finished this game, it will
    be time for your chores."
A few minutes later: "Now that your game is over, it's
    time for chores."

If your child does not respond to the announcement/command combination, use a limit setting tool from Step Five.

IN SHORT

An announcement is a statement that lets your child know she must soon stop what she is doing and do something else.

Give your child a five, ten or fifteen minute announcement before you need her to stop her play. When the time is up, call her to do the task.

Give praise when she complies.

16
The When/Then Deal

A WHEN/THEN DEAL is an agreement to give a privilege in exchange for a behavior or task. It is a low-conflict way of getting children to cooperate, because they will earn a privilege in return. You don't have to nag, because it is up to the child to do the task or not. If the child doesn't want to do it, or takes all afternoon to do it, it's on his shoulders. The only consequence of his not doing the deal is that he forfeits the privilege.

By privilege I mean an opportunity or an object, which the child likes, that the parent is willing to give. It can be any object or opportunity that seems a fair exchange to you and your child. Its negotiating power depends on its significance for the child. A little child may be thrilled to pick up toys in exchange for accompanying you to the store, for instance. Possible exchanges might be:

WHEN you are dressed, THEN you may watch TV.

WHEN you've put on your socks and shoes, THEN you
    may play outside.

WHEN you can talk in a normal voice, THEN I'll listen.

WHEN you are ready to share the game with your sister,
    THEN you may play it again.

WHEN you are in your carseat, THEN we'll drive to the
    park.

WHEN you have finished your homework, THEN I will
    take you to the library.

Use the when/then deal when your child requests a privilege or when you want to provide an incentive to do a task.

Following a child's request:

Ginny: Dad, may I ride my bike?

Dad: Sure, Ginny, when you've put away the puzzles you left
    out, then you may ride your bike.

Initiated by parent:

Mom: When your room is clean, then you may invite a friend over.

For the when/then deal to remain no-conflict, you must remain calm, ignore diversions and dawdling, and praise any attempt at all to do the task. You must also be sure to have the privilege (treat, money, etc.) or the opportunity (picnic, going to library, visit to video arcade, etc.) readily available. The privilege is not always a reward; it may simply be the activity the child wants to do next.

The child may say no, may do the task at his own (snail's) pace, or even not do his part of the deal, so when you begin to use this tool, try it out on tasks that you don't care so much about.

That way you will be calm (it won't matter really) and your child will sense he does indeed have the freedom to turn down the deal.

Practice:
Negotiating a When/Then Deal

When your child comes to you with a request—and there is something you wish the child would do (or have been nagging him to do!) such as a chore, an errand, or a favor—negotiate a when/then deal by saying you will grant the request when he's done the task.

Or, if there is a task you would like your child to do and a privilege you can offer in exchange, negotiate a when/then deal.

Remain neutral and calm. If there are protests, say simply, "It's up to you. When you're finished, you may do what you want." If the child turns down the deal and, later you need the child to do the task, use tools from Step Five.

And, as always, have the privilege your child earned readily available.

IN SHORT

A when/then deal is an agreement to give a privilege in exchange for a behavior or task. You can negotiate a when/then deal when your child requests a privilege or when you want to provide an incentive for him to do a task.

The only consequence of not doing the task is that he forfeits the privilege. Be sure to give praise for doing his part of the deal.

17
Better Behavior Chart

A BETTER BEHAVIOR CHART helps increase or decrease specific behaviors during a particular time of day, such as morning or bedtime. It is a posted record listing five or six behaviors you like and want more of from your child. The chart works well for children ages three-and-a-half to twelve. It helps inspire your child's cooperation and in a few weeks a new routine replaces the old chaos.

The Better Behavior Chart works in this way:

1. You choose behaviors you want your child to do on a daily basis.

2. For ten days of PRIVATE RECORDS you observe your child and count his successes. When you know the chart is right for your child, you GO PUBLIC.

3. You write, draw, or paste pictures of the behaviors on the chart and present the chart to your child in a short family meeting.

4. You post the chart where your child wants it. The words or pictures remind the child of his tasks, reducing your need to nag (thank you, thank you!).

5. When your child does a behavior, you immediately reward him by putting a check mark, sticker, star or happy face on the chart.

6. At the end of each day you sit down with your child, count the stars, and praise his accomplishments. Your child may earn a privilege or an inexpensive toy at the end of the week.

7. You ignore (downplay) his failures, focusing only on the terrific job your child is doing.

8. Soon your child is doing the behaviors you want willingly, often enthusiastically.

9. The chart succeeds because it is all-positive: no nagging, no punishment, no threats, just lots of recognition and celebration.

The chart for a four-year-old might look something like this:

BEHAVIOR	MON	TUES	WED	THURS	FRI
gets in bath by 6:30 with mom's help					
gets out of bath by 6:50 with mom's help with 2 reminders					
in pajamas by 7:00 all by yourself					
brushes teeth by 7:10 with dad's help					
listens to bedtime story until 7:25					
lights out (except nightlight) by 7:30					

HOW YOU SELECT CHART BEHAVIORS

1. Pick a time of day that's particularly chaotic for your family. Many families choose the before school rush, after school homework/chore time, or the ever-exhausting bedtime.

2. Select three behaviors your child does willingly during that time (four or five days a week).

3. Select two behaviors your child does occasionally during that period (two or three days a week).

4. Select one behavior your child won't do or does rarely, (once a week). A morning chart for a ten-year-old might have the following behaviors.

Three behaviors child does willingly:
    gets out of bed
    packs backpack for school
    feeds and waters pets

Two behaviors child does occasionally:
    all dressed before breakfast
    ready to leave by 8:04

One behavior child does rarely:
    face, teeth and hands (including nails) clean

Arrange the six behaviors on the chart chronologically. However, try to alternate them so that behaviors your child does willingly come before and after the more challenging behaviors. The praise he earns for the easy behaviors creates a more cooperative attitude for the difficult ones. Our example might look like this:

    out of bed by 6:50
    all dressed before breakfast at 7:05
    feeds and waters pets by 7:35
    packs backpack for school by 7:45
    face, teeth and hands (including nails) clean by 8:00
    out the door by 8:04

In arranging the chart items, don't automatically fall back on your regular schedule. Think creatively. Experiment to find the order of tasks that will enhance your child's cooperation. Because the child in this example readily packs his backpack and will easily earn a bit of praise when he does it, we list this item before the more challenging one of "face, teeth and nails." He will be more likely to cooperate with the washing up (which he hates) after he's completed packing and received some praise.

Does your child need any help? If so, include the amount of help and the helper on the chart. A young child might have the item "brushes teeth with dad's help."

Will your child need a reminder or two? What's a reasonable expectation for your child at his age? A chart item might be "gets out of bed by 6:50 with two reminders." And finally, include the time you need the behavior completed.

Place the six behaviors you have chosen on your blank chart. Here is the morning chart for the ten-year-old:

BEHAVIOR	MON	TUES	WED	THURS	FRI
out of bed by 6:50					
all dressed and comes to eat by 7:05					
feeds and waters dog and cats by 7:35					
backpack ready by 7:45 (with milk $ and anything that needs to be signed!)					
face, teeth, and hands (nails, too!) done by 8:00					
out the door by 8:04 with no reminder					
Goal: Pay day: Total earned for week:					

Note that each chart item has the time it needs to be done and the amount of help or reminders needed. You can see that the more challenging behaviors are sandwiched in between those the child does readily.

You might ask, "What about all the other behaviors? There's only one 'rarely done' behavior on the chart." There are three reasons for this. First, we are stacking the deck in favor of your child. The chart is sufficiently easy to guarantee success. Second, the atmosphere created by the chart (it's fun!) makes children more cheerful and cooperative during the selected time of day. All behaviors (chart items and others) tend to improve. And third, each week you may substitute a new behavior for one that your child is doing readily.

KEEPING PRIVATE RECORDS

Keeping private records guarantees the child's success. During private records you count the times your child does each behavior without his knowing about the chart. In my practice, I ask parents to watch their child for two weeks (usually weekdays only) before going public. I urge you to try to keep records for ten weekdays.

When your child does a behavior, record a "+" in the box. When she fails to do the behavior, mark an "0" in the box. Don't mention the item, but do continue praising any successes. Ignore or show little interest in her non-compliance, unless the situation becomes intolerable. (Then use a limit setting tool from Step Five).

At the end of each week calculate your child's success rate, that is, figure out the percentage of behaviors she completed. For example, on a six-item, five-day chart you have a potential for thirty successes or + marks. If your child earns less than fifteen (50%), the chart is too challenging. Substitute a behavior that is easier. Re-take private records until you are certain she will do at least 50% of the items.

If the success rate is over eighty percent (twenty-four items successfully done), then the chart might be too easy. You can substitute one harder item now, or after a week or two.

If your child is doing ninety percent (twenty-seven) or over, select more difficult behaviors or forget about doing a chart at all! Sounds like all you needed was to think through your morning or evening or clarify what you wanted from your child. Give a little more praise as he does what you ask and you may not need extra incentive.

GOING PUBLIC

Sit down with your child and introduce the Better Behavior Chart with the six behaviors (in words or pictures). Tell the child you have made her a chart to help things run more smoothly and that each time she does one of the behaviors you will draw her a star in the space. Tell her if she does not do a behavior, you will leave the space blank. Explain that at the end of each day you and she will count the number of stars she earns.

Rather than drawing stars you may use stickers, stamped images, happy faces, foil stars, or check marks. Ask her for ideas on what she would like put in the boxes.

Have your child select where to post the chart. The refrigerator is a popular choice, in the center of the family action, where no one will forget about it. If an older child wants the chart private, put it in her room or keep it in her dresser drawer. Use the chart to encourage, but don't draw such frequent attention that the chart becomes an agent of parental nagging.

When the child succeeds, give praise and the star or sticker immediately. You might say, "Here you go, here is your sticker for getting right out of bed when I called. Great job! Do you want to stick it on the chart yourself?"

If the child does not succeed, ignore insofar as is possible. Obviously some tasks must be done or you will never get out of the house in the morning. Use Step Five tools if you must, and leave the space blank, since the friendly reminding of the chart was not enough.

If your child is disappointed in not succeeding at an item and tries to draw your attention to it (asking for a sticker when she has not earned it), merely say to her, "Tomorrow you'll have another chance." Redirect your child's attention to her successes.

GIVING REWARDS

At the end of the day sit down with your child and count the number of stars she earned. For a young child, and for many older children, the sticker and the praise will be sufficient reward. Praise your child: "Good work! You earned three stickers today!" Share the news with other adults in the home. Let her tell an aunt or grandparent by phone.

For each success, you may give your child a token such as a poker chip which can be cashed in on Saturday for a privilege or small toy. Free or low-cost weekly rewards might include:

> trip to library (or library sponsored story hour or film)
> video rental
> picnic in the backyard
> outing to the park
> overnight at friend's
> hike
> friend or two over for special project: art project, making
>   a cardboard clubhouse
> baking cookies

Expensive rewards are not a good idea. If the toy is too valuable and requires many days and successes, the child will become discouraged. Some parents find that their child enjoys the element of surprise more than anything. They wrap a few inexpensive items in bright paper and let the child pick one.

IS THIS BRIBERY?

Many parents worry that they are, in fact, bribing and that this is harmful for their child. First of all, children may think they are doing the chore/behavior for the token, sticker, or treat. But actually they are doing it for the social reinforcer, the praise that you give when you give the token.

I discovered the importance of praise and the insignficance of prizes when a mother came to a session complaining that the charts and rewards didn't work. Ellie had earned all her stars the first week but had failed the next. I then asked the mother, "What did you say when you gave her the sticker?" She said, "Here is your sticker."

The praise and encouragement were missing. There was no smile, little eye contact, no recognition of the child's efforts. When this mother tried again, giving praise along with the stickers, the Behavior Chart began to work very successfully.

If your child will do tasks or offers to help only in exchange for money or treats, don't even introduce the idea of a physical reward other than a sticker. This is a child who needs less material and more social reward. Use only your verbal and non-verbal praise.

Don't use the Better Behavior Chart indefinitely. In fact, after three or four weeks the children tend to perform the behaviors without much reminder or other reinforcer than praise. The behaviors become habits. Parents may reinstate a chart as needed. During or following high stress times like holidays and family illness, a BBC can bring the kind of scheduling and reminder to praise that is particularly helpful. If you and your children want, you may keep the chart going, substituting one new behavior each week. Always keep a balance of easy and more challenging behaviors.

A word about siblings—most kids love the charts and if brother or sister has one they want one too. The more the merrier.

Just make sure the tasks are realistic, age-appropriate and earned with reasonable effort.

IN SHORT

The Better Behavior Chart is a posted record which reminds your child of his tasks in a fun, non-nagging way, while it reminds you to give ongoing praise as he does these tasks each day.

You can use the Better Behavior Chart to inspire cooperation and more positive family interaction during hectic mornings, afternoons, or evenings.

The Behavior Chart works because:

1. You select behaviors which the child can succeed at accomplishing.

2. You assess the amount of help and reminders needed for success.

3. You place behaviors on the chart so that your praise of the easy behaviors inspires cooperation for more difficult behaviors.

4. You reward with praise and encouragement, while giving no payoff for (ignoring) non-compliance.

To create a Better Behavior Chart you:

KEEP PRIVATE RECORDS.
Select your items. Six items or less is best.
Arrange them chronologically and so that success builds
    on success.
Add the number of reminders, help needed, and time for
    task to be completed.
Observe and record behaviors for ten days.
    When your child has earned fifteen stars (50% or
    more per week),

GO PUBLIC.
Sit down with your child and introduce the Behavior
    Chart.
Tell the child that the chart will help things run more
    smoothly in the morning.
Tell her each time she does one of the behaviors you will
    give her a star in the space. If she fails to do a
    behavior, you will leave the space on the chart blank.
Explain that at the end of each day you'll count the
    number of stars she earns.
Have your child select where to post the chart.
Every time a task is completed, give your child a sticker
    and praise her.
Give an older child tokens that can be cashed in for a
    privilege on Saturday.
At the end of the day, sit down with the child and count
    the total number of stickers earned.
Share the results with other adults in the home.

Use the chart to inspire.

When the child succeeds, give positive attention immediately.

If the child does not do a task in the time allotted, ignore it as best you can. (Use Step Five limit setting if you must and leave the chart space blank.)

If your child is disappointed that he didn't get a star, say only, "Tomorrow you'll have another chance."

Redirect your child's attention to the successes he has already achieved.

Follow though with lots of praise and, if you like, weekly rewards.

Step 5: Setting Limits

You are the parent. It's your job to provide the limits your child needs and—though he doesn't realize it—wants. To feel the world is safe, he needs to know that mom and dad are in control. You not only have the right, you have the responsibility to take charge and set limits on misbehavior.

In this section you will learn techniques for setting limits to stop intolerable behaviors. You will see how to apply what you have already learned to reduce intolerable behaviors. And you will learn about Commands, the Broken Record Technique, Warnings and Consequences, Time-outs, Family Meetings, and how to set limits in public. All of these can help you provide consistent and appropriate reactions to all of your child's intolerable behaviors and build a more cooperative atmosphere in your home.

18
Using the Tools You Know

It's no fun barking orders all day long. But let's face it, we do sound like drill sergeants at times. What are the alternatives? Being overly permissive keeps us from being the bad guy, but may result in children who are dependent, manipulative or lacking in self-discipline. And unless you want your kids in your bed all night, in pajamas until noon, late for school (with you late to work), and up until midnight, you need to set some limits. Let's start by eliminating intolerable behavior with techniques you already know.

You have learned to look at behaviors and decide if they are behaviors you like, dislike, or find intolerable.

You have learned to increase behaviors you like by giving positive attention—praising.

You have learned to decrease behaviors you dislike by removing attention—ignoring.

You have learned to invite cooperation rather than demand it—with announcements, choices, and the when/then deal.

You have learned to create a more cooperative atmosphere for chores and stressful times of day with the Better Behavior Chart.

Before I introduce the limit setting tools, I must stress the importance of learning and applying the tools in Steps One, Two, Three, and Four. You may feel frustrated. You may think, "His behaviors are intolerable all day long! I need discipline tools!" But I must ask you not to use the limit setting tools without mastering praise and ignore. Why?

1. If you attempt to punish without learning to praise you will find your children's behavior getting worse. Remember, children will go for punishment if they cannot figure out how to earn positive attention. If you do not teach them how to earn your praise through cooperation, they will continue to misbehave to get negative attention (punishment).

In homes where praising becomes a habit, the quality of family interaction improves considerably. Everyone seems to like each other more and enjoy each other more. In this climate, much misbehavior decreases on its own. With praising, less discipline is needed.

When a child finally does cooperate after misbehaving, you must be willing and able to praise him. After the punishment (time-out, consequence) is over and your child has stopped the intolerable behavior or begun to do a behavior you like, you need to give him a way back into the family. Holding grudges and keeping cold silences serve no purpose. A child must know the world doesn't end when he has broken a rule or angered his parents. He must know how to begin again to earn your praise and encouragement and you must be ready to give it.

Many of our limit setting techniques, such as family meeting or giving commands, require praising to be effective. They will not work without it. You must be able and willing to praise before attempting to set limits.

2. You also must be able to ignore before you attempt to set limits. Ignoring is an effective tool for decreasing undesirable behaviors, often quickly and thoroughly. You should always try the ignore/praise combination before you resort to other measures. Ignoring is also an essential part of most limit setting tactics. You must ignore when your child argues about a consequence, complains about a command, makes diversionary remarks during a family meeting, tantrums in response to a time-out, and so forth. If you are unable and unwilling to ignore, your limit setting efforts will be wasted.

3. Limit setting tools are most effective when used sparingly. They can be overused. For example, if you are giving time-outs every day, or several times a day, soon they will lose their impact. By using praising, ignoring and invitations to cooperate to reduce the majority of undesirable behaviors, you keep your limit setting tools as a powerful back-up.

Let's review how to apply the tools you already know to intolerable behaviors:

1. Identify the intolerable behavior.

2. Define the opposite of the intolerable behavior (a desirable behavior).

3. Watch for and praise the smallest step in the right direction towards the desirable behavior.

4. Remove your attention from the irritating, obnoxious parts of the intolerable behavior. Ignore, down play, distract, change the subject, show interest in other things. If the child is three or over, you can announce

you will be ignoring the behavior.

5. Use the ignore/praise combination if one child does a behavior you dislike.

6. Use one of the invitations to cooperate.
    Make a when/then deal (with the "when" being a realistic expectation), offer a choice, or use a Better Behavior Chart to improve cooperation during high stress times of day.

And finally, if the above approaches do not completely eliminate the intolerable behaviors, use the limit setting tools that will be presented next: commands, warnings and consequences, broken record, family meetings, and time-outs.

Let's take the common problem of sibling fighting. Alex and Jenny start playing a game and soon they are arguing and accusing each other of cheating. It ends in hitting and screaming. Let's see how their parents would use the tools.

1. Identify the behavior which has become intolerable.
    Alex and Jenny fighting, squabbling, screaming and hitting.

2. Identify the opposite of the intolerable behavior—what you want in its place.
    That's easy: sharing, getting along well, playing fairly, winning without bragging and losing without a tantrum, coming to me for help if one hits the other instead of slugging back, using their words instead of their fists.

3. Watch for and praise the smallest movement in the right direction.
    That would be about five minutes of non-squabbling play. At the start they do pretty well. I could say, "I like how you two are

playing that game so well."

4. Announce you're going to ignore the irritating behaviors in the situation.

Although it will be hard, I suppose I could ignore the bickering, at least until they start hitting. I could say, "I am not going to listen to your arguing. I am going to let you two work things out."

5. Use the praise/ignore combination when one child starts an intolerable behavior, such as hitting.

If Jenny hit Alex and instead of hitting back, Alex called me, I could say, "I'm glad you didn't hit back, Alex," and I could ask if he wanted to play in my room, by himself, or outside away from his sister. All this time I would ignore Jenny, even though I'd feel like giving her a lecture! If he chose to keep playing with her, I would keep an eye out for a while. I'd praise if they got along for even three minutes, saying something like, "Great job getting along, you two."

6. Use an invitation to cooperate.

Make a when/then deal:

Before things get out of hand, I could say, "When you two have played together nicely one half-hour—that means keeping your hands to yourself and using indoor-voices—then you may have one half hour of TV or computer time." Those are no-cost privileges they like and that I'd be able to give right away.

Offer a choice.

I could say, "You children have a choice–you may play together or play separately. But if you choose to play together, you may not hit or scream. If you do, you must play in separate areas." For instance, Jenny could play outside or use my room and Alex could play in the kids' room. I know that they will play together better if they think it's a privilege they might lose.

Make a BBC (Better Behavior Chart).

I could use the time of day the children play together, say from 4:30 until dinnertime at 6:30. I've seen them play together for 20 to 30 minutes at a time before the bickering and hitting start. I could divide that period of time into half-hours. I'd be sure to reward any success with praise. I'd call the children to the chart, give stickers or draw happy faces in the box. If they failed during that individual time period, I'd leave the box blank. My chart items would be:

Keep hands to self 4:30 to 5:00 with one reminder
Keep hands to self 5:00 to 5:30 with one reminder
Keep hands to self 5:30 to 6:00 with one reminder
Keep hands to self 6:00 to 6:30 with one reminder

NOTE: If Alex and Jenny cannot play for that long without squabbling, their parents should use shorter segments of time— twenty, ten or even five minutes.

IN SHORT

Before you resort to firmer limit setting measures, first try out the tools you already know to stop intolerable behaviors:

1. Identify the intolerable behavior.

2. Identify the opposite of the intolerable behavior— what you want in its place.

3. Watch for and praise the smallest movement in the right direction.

4. Announce you are going to ignore the irritating behavior.

5. Use the praise/ignore combination when one child starts an intolerable behavior that is not harmful.

6. Use an invitation to cooperate:
    Make a when/then deal. Follow-through with the privilege right away.   Praise when you get even a small amount of cooperation.
    Offer a choice.
    Make a BBC (Better Behavior Chart).

And if the above approaches do not completely eliminate the intolerable behavior, read on.

19
Commands

The first and simplest limit setting tool is the COMMAND statement. It is so effective that a command followed by praise for the smallest step in the right direction may be all that you need to get your child to start or stop a behavior.

"Share your trucks with your brother." (start sharing)

"Stop throwing rocks at the squirrel right now." (stop throwing rocks)

HOW TO GIVE EFFECTIVE COMMANDS

EYES — Establish eye contact. Have your child come to you or you go to your child. If necessary, call her name until she looks at you, say "thank you," and then give the command. (The "thank-you" will take her a bit by surprise and she may comply in spite of herself).

WORDS — Name the behavior you want your child to stop or start. It helps your child know exactly what you want.
Wrong: Stop that!
Correct: Put those scissors on the table.

It is usually better to name the behavior you want, rather than the unwanted behavior.

O.K.:   Stop patting the baby so roughly!
Even better: Touch the baby gently, please.

The danger in naming the behavior you want stopped is that it also may remind the child of the rough behavior, perhaps challenging her to repeat it, and certainly reinforcing it with attention. Naming the desired behavior tells her exactly what to do. It gives the child a chance to comply immediately and gives you an opportunity to praise her.

BE SURE TO PHRASE YOUR COMMANDS AS A STATEMENT AND NOT A QUESTION. Don't ask a question unless you will accept a "no" for an answer.

Don't ask:	When you mean:
Don't you think it's time for bed?	It's time for bed.
Would you like to take your bath?	Take your bath now, please.
Are you hungry for supper?	Come in for supper.

VOICE — Your tone should be neutral, firm, but not angry.

No matter how angry you feel, try to remain calm. I am not saying you should hide your anger from your child, just that your commands will be more effective if you appear to be in control.

Remember that the goal is to have the child do what you are asking. Children will be more apt to hear the command and follow it if you are firm and in control.

Try this experiment. By yourself, yell a command ("Go to bed!") angrily and at the top of your lungs, arms flailing if you tend toward the dramatic. Next, speak the same command in a firm calm, indoor voice, without the anger. Feel the difference. Which one would be more effective with your child? Not in scaring her of course, but in communicating how serious you are that she go to bed. I think you'll find there is great power in using a firm, but neutral tone.

Certainly, in a situation of danger—your toddler comes in with the scissors—you will raise your voice, even shout. Don't lose any sleep over it. The occasional loud warning will be all the more effective if you have been practicing a neutral voice for your day-to-day, non-emergency commands.

Be realistic. Sometimes your child needs a reminder or even two before she will comply with the command. The reminder is given in a neutral voice, with eye contact, and without anger. However, after two reminders you are nagging. And you have a right not to be a nag. Go directly to the next level of limit setting.

TAKE YOURSELF SERIOUSLY

For a command to be effective you must say it as if you mean it. A child who feels you are committed is more likely to cooperate with you. To appear serious you must be unambiguous. Sometimes that's difficult. Perhaps your children are playing outside and it is near dusk. You are thinking, "They're having such a good time, I might as well let them play longer." On the other hand, you know how rushed bedtime can be, how irritable everyone gets when they're tired.

If you call your children inside when you are torn about it, your command, "It's time to come in now" will lack commitment. The children will sense your reluctance and may ignore you. It's best to make up your mind, commit yourself to wanting a behavior started or stopped, then give the command.

Practice:
Giving Effective Commands

Refer to your list of intolerable behaviors. This may be a fairly short list at the moment, if you have used the praise/ignore combination. A list of intolerables might look something like this:

> throwing objects when angry
> jumping on furniture
> pulling the cat's tail
> refusing to go to bed
> hitting brother
> leaving the house or yard
> spitting

Pick one behavior to work on, for example, leaving the yard.

Identify the behavior you want in its place–staying in the yard.

Select a command.

Name the behavior you want, rather than what you want stopped, if possible. Don't use a question. Examples:

> "You must ask me before you can leave our yard."
> "Stay in our yard."
> "The rule is: no leaving our yard."

The next time the target behavior occurs:

> Go to your child.
> Make eye contact.
> Use a firm, neutral tone.
> Give the command.

Each time you want a behavior started or stopped repeat this process. Soon it will become second nature for you to calmly give firm, direct commands.

I find that parents immediately increase the amount of cooperation they get once they can give commands effectively. This may be because they have used an indirect style in the past. They ask questions, rather than give statements. They are ambiguous about setting limits, not liking to say "no." They don't like to be the bad guy and postpone setting a limit until things have gone too far. By learning to give an effective command they feel stronger and are more powerful. As a single mother of a large family put it: "I feel like I'm the mother now." You may need to give a reminder or two, but you don't have to be a nag. After two reminders, give a warning of a consequence!

IN SHORT

A command is a simple statement to your child to start or stop a behavior. To give commands effectively:

> Make eye contact with your child.
> Name the behavior you want.
> Make a statement, do not ask a question.
> Use a neutral, firm tone.
> Give a reminder if necessary.
> Take yourself seriously (so will your child).

20
The Broken Record Technique

The BROKEN RECORD technique, the simple repeating of the command, is a wonderful tool for combating arguing or D.T.'s (diversionary tactics). Children often want to divert our attention from the command we just gave. Here Josh uses D.T.'s.

Dad: It's time for bed, Josh.

Josh: But it's only 8:30.

Dad: 8:30 is late enough.

Josh: No one else in my class has to go to bed at 8:30.

Dad: Oh, I'm sure plenty of them do.

Josh: No, they don't. Everybody gets to watch TV 'til 9:30.

Dad: Well, maybe that's true, but you're not everybody.

Josh: It's not fair.

Dad: It may not seem fair, Josh, but your mother and I think that 8:30 is an appropriate bedtime for an eight-year-old.

Josh: If Mom says I can stay up 'til 9:30, can I?

and on and on. You get the picture.

Put yourself in Josh's shoes for a moment. See how it feels when his Dad uses the broken record technique:

Dad: It's time for bed, Josh.
Josh: But it's only 8:30.
Dad: It's time for bed.
Josh: No one else in my class has to go to bed at 8:30.
Dad: It's time for bed.
Josh: Everybody but me gets to watch TV 'til 9:30
Dad: It's time for bed.
Josh: It's not fair.
Dad: It's time for bed.
Josh: Why do you keep saying that?
Dad: It's time for bed.
Josh: All right, all right, just stop saying that stupid "It's time for bed."
Dad: Thank you, Josh. I'll be up in a minute to kiss you good night.

The Dad here is, in fact, ignoring Josh. It's as if he is saying, "No matter what you say, you still have to go to bed now—I'm going to ignore every argument you come up with." Because the child is getting no payoff, he will eventually stop the behavior (arguing). The parent does not have to search for arguments. He can simply repeat the command. Parents love this technique. They don't have to get angry, don't have to yell, don't have to out argue their bright, resourceful, energetic children. They remain calm and the child runs out of steam.

Warning: If your child uses the broken record technique
       on you (even though in this age of tapes and CD's

they have no idea what a broken record sounds like) stop immediately. They have won. Go on to another level of limit setting.

Example:

Mom: Time for bed, Josh.
Josh: No.
Mom: It's time for bed.
Josh: No.
Mom: It's time for bed.
Josh: No.
Mom: [knows her limits, uses a warning of a consequence]

IN SHORT

The broken record technique is the simple repeating of a command when your child tries to divert you with arguments. To be effective you should remain very calm and not change a word of your message. If your child does the broken record back to you, give up. Use a warning of a consequence (Chapter 21).

Example:

Mom: It's time for your bath.
Child: But I'm not dirty.
Mom: It's time for your bath.
Child: I want to do it later.
Mom: It's time for your bath.
Child: You said I could have lots of time to play.
Mom: It's time for your bath.
Child: OK already! I'm going.
Mom: Thank you.

21
Warnings and Consequences

A WARNING is a statement of a CONSEQUENCE you will give your child unless he starts or stops a certain behavior.

Use a warning of a consequence when your child ignores your command and you need to use another level of limit setting. Be sure to name the behavior you want stopped and name the consequence which you will give. A minimal consequence is usually effective.

If the behavior continues you must follow through with the consequence immediately. A consequence is:

The loss of a privilege or object
which has meaning for the child
over which the parent has control
that the parent is willing to take away.

Example:

Mia is bouncing the ball off the ceiling inside the house.

Parent gives command:
"Mia, take the ball outside, please."
Mia ignores parent.

Parent gives reminder:
"Mia, I said 'Take the ball outside.'"
Mia ignores parent, keeps bouncing ball.

Parent gives warning:
"Take the ball outside now, Mia, or I will put the ball away for fifteen minutes." (Not: "Stop that or else!")

Notice that this fits our definition of consequence:

LOSS OF A PRIVILEGE — Use of ball for a short time.
WHICH HAS MEANING FOR CHILD — She's playing
    with ball now and doesn't want to stop.
PARENT HAS CONTROL OF PRIVILEGE — Parent
    could easily intercept ball and hide it.
PARENT IS WILLING TO TAKE AWAY — It's a great
    choice, directly connected to the intolerable behavior.

Unless it's dangerous, always try to give a warning before giving a consequence. It spells out clearly to the child what he can expect if he continues the behavior. It also gives him an opportunity to take responsibility for his own actions. He can continue and be punished or he can stop the behavior and get praise. If the child earns a consequence and then does the behavior again a little later, you don't need to give a second warning.

Sometimes it is hard to think of appropriate consequences. In general it is best if you can link the consequence to the problem behavior for so-called logical or natural consequences. An earlier bedtime tomorrow for refusing bedtime tonight is a good example of linking.

Be careful in your choice of consequences. The idea is to set a limit, not devastate. No child should lose a party. Don't ever take away your three-year-old's security blanket or a twelve-year-old's scouting trip he has looked forward to for weeks. And never, ever take away a privilege that your child has worked hard to earn.

A short term consequence is more effective than a long term one, although parents tend to think that grounding their child for a week or removing the video games for two weeks will guarantee improved behavior. Children quickly forget about the incident (they remember the consequence but not the offense). A consequence more than a day long is wasted energy for you all. Also, the longer the consequence, the fewer options you have. Use of the telephone might be your only good consequence for a pre-adolescent. If you deny her use of the telephone for two weeks, what can you use if you need a consequence tomorrow?

What impact can a short term loss of privilege have? Think of the impact if you turned off the TV in the last two minutes of a tied game or denied a teenager even fifteen minutes of music or made a child go to bed ten minutes early. Who needs two weeks?

More importantly, a short consequence can help teach self-control. It gives the child the opportunity to try again soon, not several days later. Let's take our example of the little girl Mia bouncing the ball in the house.

Mia bounces her ball after her mother has given her a warning. Her mother holds out her hand for the ball. Mia reluctantly places the ball in her mother's hand. Her mother says, "Thank you, Mia, I'll give it back to you in fifteen minutes."

Her mother sets a kitchen timer for fifteen minutes. Initially angry and sulking, Mia soon absorbs herself playing with another toy. When the timer rings her mother gives the ball back to Mia and says, "Here's your ball back, Mia. You may play with it outside now."

Correctly, Mia's mother does not take this opportunity—tempting though it may be—to lecture. At most, she redirects Mia's play outside. There is no anger, no reproach in her voice. Instead she is inviting her back into the family. Mia may resume sulking, may knock the ball out of her mother's hand, may turn and walk away, or may lie on the floor and have a full blown tantrum. All these Mia's mother ignores.

When she does take the ball outside to play, her mother praises her. Even if she is angry, rather than hold a grudge which is an emotional punishment, the parent says, "Thank you, Mia, for playing outside with the ball." The child knows the punishment is over and understands how to continue getting attention from her parent. The incident ends with the child cooperating and the parent praising. This positive attention will enable the desirable behavior to continue and keep the undesirable behavior from returning. Firm, fair, short-term limit setting can result in helping the child gain self-control and can permanently change a behavior.

Some effective consequences are:

> loss of the use of radio or tape recorder for fifteen minutes
> earlier bedtime (twenty minutes)
> removal of toy for five to twenty minutes depending on age
> must come inside from play for five minutes
> may not play with sibling or friend for eight minutes
> loss of use of phone for one evening
> loss of planned outing (be sure to warn first)
> loss of use of bicycle, skateboard for a morning
> loss of use of TV, computer, video game for ten minutes
> five minute time-out

IN SHORT

To stop an unwanted behavior and start a behavior you like use the following steps:

Give a command.
Give a reminder.
Give a warning of a consequence.
Follow through with the consequence.
Praise when you see a behavior you like in its place.

22
Time-out

TIME-OUT is a consequence that can be used effectively for children three to twelve years old. It is portable. You can use time-out at grandma's house or at the neighbors or even in the grocery store. Time-out is very helpful when you cannot quickly think of an appropriate consequence.

You use time-out in this way:

1. Pick a place in the home for time-out. I suggest a chair in a corner that has no potential for greater trouble: no wall paper to tear, no outlet to stick things in. It should not be closed off (especially not a bathroom where there are medicines or breakable bottles). Though some parents find that time-out works well in the child's bedroom, most children will start playing with their toys. This is hardly a punishment (and after all time-out is a form of punishment). A time-out corner close to the family action

where you can keep an eye on your child is ideal.

2. Pick a length of time for time-out. One minute for each year of the child's age works well. Five minutes is often plenty for a first offense even for an older child. If the behavior you dislike continues, each time-out may be increased by a minute or so. Use a kitchen timer. Show it to your child. Tell her time-out will be over when the timer dings.

3. Introduce the time-out in a short family meeting. Sit down with your child. Name the intolerable behavior, tell how you feel about it, and say that you have a plan to help her stop the behavior. Show her where the chair will be placed and how the timer will be set. It is very helpful to do a practice run. Most children cooperate readily with the meeting and the practice because it is not yet a punishment. This meeting should last ten minutes or less.

4. When an intolerable behavior starts, give a warning of time-out. Remember, it is always best to give the child the opportunity to exhibit some self control and stop the behavior herself. Give her a chance by warning her she is about to earn a time-out. If she stops the behavior, praise her.

Example:

> Eight-year-old Larry plays on the garage roof. Larry's father has explained how dangerous it is, but the reminders have had no effect. Larry's dad gives a warning of a time-out:

Dad: Larry, if I find you on the roof again you will have time-out. Do you understand?

Larry: Yes, Dad.

Dad: Thank you. I'm glad it's clear to you.

If the behavior continues, follow through with giving time-out.

Larry: [climbs onto the garage roof]
Dad: Larry, you must come in from play for an eight minute
       time-out. This will be the time-out chair here. [he places a
       chair in a corner of the dining area facing the wall] I will
       set the timer for the eight minutes. [Larry sits down]
       Thank you, Larrry. When the timer rings your time-out
       will be done.

When time-out is over, make a simple announcement in a neutral voice, such as "Your time out is over now, you may go play." Some children will continue to sit in the corner sulking. Ignore it for while. Occasionally give a little invitation back to family life such as, "Would you like to help me set the table for dinner?" or ask the child's opinion about something. Do not sit down beside the child and try to coax him out of the chair.

Nor should you give a lecture at the end of time-out. Some parents, perhaps out of guilt or discomfort at having to give a punishment, use the post time-out moment to explain why they gave the time-out or try to extract a promise of better behavior. This lecture will actually increase the child's sulking or repetition of the intolerable behavior. In our busy daily schedule we often do not find the time to have a real heart-to-heart talk unless a problem behavior has occurred. Make sure you are looking for and finding desirable behaviors to encourage on a daily basis, so that the child knows exactly how to get your attention in positive ways.

A child may resist time-out with:	Combat these with:
diversionary tactics (D.T.'s)	ignoring
arguments	the broken record technique
down-right refusal	choice of time-out or
	another consequence

Here is an example of a mother giving a twelve-year-old a time-out. Notice she starts with a when/then deal:

Mom: Eddie, you've earned a ten minute time-out. Use this chair. When you are seated, I'll start the timer.

Eddie: [screams] It's not fair.

Mom: [ignores diversions, in calm voice uses broken record] When you are in the seat, I'll start the timer.

Eddie: [remains standing for thirty seconds]

Mom: [gets timer, returns and waits without comment; there are several moments of stand-off while Mother pretends she has all the time in the world]

Eddie: [moves toward chair slowly] I don't see why I have to sit in the stupid chair. It wasn't my fault the lamp broke. [slowly collapses into chair]

Mom: Thank you, Eddie. I'll start the timer now. [shows him timer, turns it to ten minutes]

Eddie: [squirms a bit, mumbles, but stays in chair]

Mom: Thank you, Eddie. [ignores his squirming and mumbling until timer rings] Your time out is over, Eddie. You may play or come help me now.

Eddie protests slightly, mumbles and dawdles going into time-out, probably as a face-saving device. His mother tolerates the squirming and mumbling. If his mother had tried to argue with him or hold him to an impossible standard of absolute quiet, there would have been more arguing. Eddie's mother wisely uses ignoring, the broken record technique, and a calm, neutral manner, and he finally complies.

If Eddie had refused to sit down, his mother could have stood, waiting, and repeated, "When you are seated, I will start the timer." Some parents find it effective to add a minute or so of time to the time-out if the protests continue. If your child absolutely refuses, resort to the back-up plan.

THE BACK-UP PLAN

You don't want to physically carry your child to time-out, so it's helpful to have a back-up plan. If your child refuses to take a time-out, offer him a choice. Eddie's mother might have offered:

> "You may have a ten minute time-out now or when your dad gets home we will both give you a fifteen minute time-out."

> "You may have a ten minute time-out now or go to bed fifteen minutes early tonight."

> "Either take a ten minute time-out or lose all your TV time tonight."

If your child chooses the alternative to time-out, be sure you follow-through with the consequence.

USE TIME-OUT SPARINGLY

Time-out is very effective, but if you are using it every day all day long it will rapidly lose its impact. Use it for one or two behaviors only, unless these behaviors occur rarely. Remember that every time the child does the intolerable behavior, she must be given time-out.

IN SHORT

Time-out is a simple, portable, ever-ready consequence. Use time-out this way:

1. Pick a place for time-out. A chair in a corner close to the family action is ideal.

2. Pick a time for time-out. One minute per age of child or less is fine for the first offense.

3. Use a kitchen timer.

4. As with every consequence, use a warning before giving a time-out.

5. If the behavior repeats, give the time-out.

6. Use ignoring, the broken record, and choice of a greater consequence if your child resists time-out.

7. When the time-out is over, do not lecture. Simply say, "Your time-out is over. Thank you."

23
Solving Problems with a Family Meeting

A FAMILY MEETING is a gathering of the family for the purpose of sharing news, making decisions, enjoying each other or solving problems.

The agenda can include announcements of upcoming school events, coordinating everyone's schedule for the week, deciding who will do what chores, planning a family outing or vacation, or just a popcorn party.

For some families, their Sunday dinner or Saturday breakfast serves as a family meeting. Other families enjoy more formal meetings, which can be good lessons in democratic participation. They post an agenda on the refrigerator door and anyone can write down an issue for discussion. They rotate the role of chairperson so that even the toddler can experience having power in the family.

Although I would not use meal time as a problem solving session, I do encourage frequent opportunities for family catching up. When you have a specific problem within the family with one or more members, use the following approach.

1.   DEFINE THE PROBLEM. This is a little tricky. Prior to the meeting, parents should decide why the behavior is a problem.

Let's say the Hampton family rule is "be home by six o'clock." When ten-year-old Nicole comes in from riding her bike at six-thirty, it raises any one of several issues:

It's dangerous to be riding her bike in the dark.
She'll be late for dinner which is at 6 o'clock.
It makes her bedtime later.
Her parents would like to spend time with her.
She needs to do her chores or homework.
Her parents just want her home at six.

2.   THINK OF POSSIBLE SOLUTIONS. In the meeting the children may present solutions, but parents will benefit from having a few workable ideas thought out in advance. The solution should be tied to the problem, of course.

The Hamptons could wrestle with these possibilities:

Put a light on the bike and have Nicole wear white so she
    could be seen in the dark.
Move dinner later so she could play outside longer.
Move bedtime later so she could play outside longer.
Have Nicole do her chores in the morning.
Have Nicole do homework right after school.
Insist on the six o'clock curfew, but allow a privilege.

and so on...

3. PLAN A MEETING TIME. Make it convenient for everyone if possible–late Sunday afternoon, Friday night, Saturday morning.

4. SIT DOWN WITH THE FAMILY (or just the children involved in the problem) in a quiet place. Thank everyone for coming.

5. MAINTAIN A CALM, NEUTRAL, AND FIRM TONE. Be prepared to ignore all diversionary tactics, sulking, and talking back.

6. STATE THE PROBLEM SIMPLY, CLEARLY, AND BRIEFLY, just the facts. Avoid labeling, name-calling, criticism and sarcasm.

7. ASK FOR IDEAS THAT MIGHT SOLVE THE SITUATION. Praise constructive ideas and ignore clearly uncooperative suggestions.

8. COME TO AN AGREEMENT THROUGH COMPROMISE (finding a middle ground) OR NEGOTIATION (mutual exchange of something that you want for something that she wants). The Hampton family could choose to compromise:

Parents want Nicole home at six.
Nicole wants to come home at six-thirty.
They compromise on six-fifteen.

Or they could choose to negotiate an exchange based on the identified problem with the behavior:

PROBLEM: Parents want more time with Nicole.
EXCHANGE: Nicole could give up her TV time to visit

with them—for the privilege of coming in at six-thirty.

PROBLEM: Biking after dark is unsafe.
EXCHANGE: Nicole could put lights and reflectors on the bike, promise to wear a white sweatshirt, and avoid riding the busiest streets—for the privilege of coming in at six-thirty.

PROBLEM: Six-thirty is too late to do homework or chores.
EXCHANGE: Nicole could do chores and homework right after school, and come in at six-thirty.

PROBLEM: Parents want Nicole in the house for all the above reasons.
EXCHANGE: Parents could allow Nicole to have friends in, or she could have extra play time on the weekends—in exchange for Nicole coming in at six.

9. SET A DATE FOR A FOLLOW-UP MEETING three days to a week later to assess how the agreement is working.

10. PRAISE FAMILY MEMBERS FOR COMING to the meeting and working out the problem.

11. Very soon have a family meeting that is pure fun!

IN SHORT

You may use family meetings to address behaviors which have become intolerable. Use the following format:

1. Define the problem and think of possible solutions.
2. Set a meeting.
3. Maintaining a calm tone, state the problem clearly and ask for ideas.
4. Come to an agreement through compromise or negotiation.
5. Assess the situation in a follow-up meeting.

And remember that a great way to increase positive family feeling is to have frequent get-togethers where good times, ideas and information are shared.

24
Setting Limits in Public

"Look at that lousy parent!"
"What an obnoxious kid!"
"How dare he slap that child!"
"Boy, that kid deserves a spanking!"

The hardest thing about setting limits in public places is the "public." Our child misbehaves and we have to untangle the mess with strangers watching! Of course, no child or parent is immune. No matter how alone you feel at that moment, every parent has faced this or a similar situation. All children go through times of being nearly unbearable in public:

running into the street
refusing to get into the car or to put on a seat belt
touching breakables in stores

> whining for drinks, video games and gumballs
> bickering with sister or brother
> wanting to be carried
> having a kicking and screaming tantrum
> throwing food and kicking under the table in restaurants

You have a right to shop, eat out, and do your errands in (relative) peace. You have a right to reasonable behavior from your children in public, as well as in the home. And the "public" should have rights too. You don't want your child intruding on the enjoyment of others as they attempt to shop, eat out, do their errands, and so forth.

So what do you do with an unruly child in public? Remember that you have a right, in fact a responsibility, to set limits. Remember that it is okay to use firm, non-physical limit setting in public, whether it be a time-out or the loss of a privilege.

Know your limits—and your child's. A four-year-old will not be very cooperative if he is tired, hungry and in the third hour of errand-running. Taking a two-year-old out to dinner can be a monumental horror. Plan ahead. Think about what will help your child during those stressful times:

> Keep healthy snacks stashed to give to a cranky, hungry child.
> Bring along a small box of crayons and pad of paper or other small emergency toys.
> Bring a pre-teen helper along with you.
> Don't try to accomplish all errands in one trip—it may be more convenient, but more stressful too.
> Trade off baby-sitting with a neighbor. You take care of his kids for two hours in the morning in exchange for your being able to run two hours of child-free errands that afternoon.
> Do your errands in order of necessity, so that you can

choose to leave some until another day if you must.
Stop in the park or by a city fountain with fast-food or a
homemade picnic. Get a second wind.

If your child is going through a phase of in-public tantrums, for a week or two go to all efforts to leave him with family or friends when you must run errands. Don't take him out to eat at all. Then use praise/ignore and the when/then deal to inspire cooperative behavior when you renew errand running with your child. You might say:

If you are a good cooperator for me in the grocery store,
(and that means staying where I can see you all the time)
I will play a game with you for twenty minutes when we
get home.

And then praise every few minutes or so in the store as he keeps to your side.

USING TIME-OUT IN PUBLIC

Time-out can be used in public. It works the same as it does at home.

1. Before you leave the house or while driving, REMIND YOUR CHILDREN OF THE RULES you need followed, such as:
    "Keep your hands to yourself in the back seat of the car."
    "Stay in the car seat (or in the seat belt)."
    "Stay in my sight in the store."
    "Keep hands off items on the shelves."

2. MAKE A WHEN/THEN DEAL, such as:
    "If you follow these rules, we will rent a video for this evening when we get back."

3. WARN THEM that you will give a time-out if a rule is broken. Your child will know you're serious if you've brought the kitchen timer!

"This is your warning, if you run away from me once more, you will have a time out."

4. PICK A PLACE FOR TIME-OUT.

As you enter the store (or wherever) glance about. Select the best place to give a time-out if you have to. A restroom is the easiest. Some parents walk their child back to the car and use that. If there are two adults and several children, one adult can walk the child outside the building (or into the restroom). I have used a corner of the grocery or department store, picking the spot that looks the least traveled. Be creative. Almost any space will work. The success of the time-out depends more on your neutrality and firmness.

5. PICK A LENGTH OF TIME for time-out.

Keep it short. Your child will be fairly amazed you are doing this in public, maybe even more embarrassed than you. A minute or two should be sufficient.

6. IF THE BEHAVIOR CONTINUES, FOLLOW THROUGH with giving time-out. Ignore diversionary tactics and use the broken record for arguing.

"All right, come with me to this corner. Sit here for one minute. I'll tell you when your time is up."

If your child resists, give a choice of a time-out now or a longer time-out later, or another equally fitting consequence for when you return home.

"You have a choice: to take your time-out or lose the video tape tonight."

7.   ANNOUNCE TIME-OUT IS OVER in a neutral voice.
Do not lecture. Just say,
"Your time-out is over. Thank-you."

8.   PRAISE as soon as your child does another behavior you like
or refrains from the intolerable behavior.
"I like how you are staying where I can see you."

SECRET WEAPON: THE TRIAL RUN

I drove up in front of my house one day to see my neighbor
firmly leading her daughter up the steps. She announced that she
was bringing Lily home to stay with daddy and would be
returning to the market to get the groceries.

Errand-running together is a treat for her and her daughter.
Beth works full-time and their trips to the market, bank, and dry
cleaners are ways to spend time together. Lily had demanded to
sit in the cart with the groceries. When her mom said she could
not (too many groceries), Lily had created a big scene. Beth gave
a warning that if Lily did not stop, she would take her home.

Lily did not stop. Her mother then left the full shopping cart
and brought Lily straight home. She deposited Lily with her
father and returned to the grocery store a few miles away.

I tell this example over and over because my wise neighbor
never has had to do that again. Unlike so many parents who
threaten to leave the store or the restaurant, Beth followed
through on her warning and established great credibility with
Lily. Lily now knows that if she is given a warning of a
consequence, she had better think seriously about stopping what
she is doing, because her mom will follow through.

You can set limits in the market (if you need to leave, have
the clerk put aside the cart), in the car (stop the car every time the
intolerable behavior occurs or drive directly home), and in

restaurants. In fact, plan an outing, such as the one below, to build up your credibility. This is a non-stress trial run, but only you know it's a trial. Use this plan:

1. Pick a fast food or other inexpensive restaurant that the children like.

2. Announce you are all going out to eat and remind the children of the rules:
   Food stays on the plate, fork, or in the mouth (no
      throwing or spitting food).
   Keep your feet to yourself (no kicking under the table).
   Stay seated (no running around the restaurant).

3. Warn that if the rules are broken, you will all leave the restaurant immediately.

4. Go to the restaurant. Order coffee, tea, or water (something you can walk away from easily). Let the children order foods they like.

5. Praise behaviors you like: "Great job..." "Thank you for..." "I like how you two are..."

6. When a child breaks a rule, stand up and say calmly, "You broke the rule. Let's go." You take everyone home. Leave the food on the table or they can grab what they can, depending on your tolerance for in-car mess.

7. You ignore their protests, graciously accept apologies, and tell the children they will have another chance some day to try again. Don't worry so much about the other children. Yes, their rights have been stepped on, but this creates some peer pressure which also will have impact on the offending child.

Remember, most likely you will not have to do this more than once. It's well worth the effort. Happy errands!

IN SHORT

You have a right to some peace, even on outings and errands. Use time-out when you need to set a limit. Use a trial run to build up your credibility as a parent who will follow-though with a consequence.

THE TIME-OUT PLAN:

1. Remind your child of the rules .
2. Make a when/then deal to inspire cooperation.
3. Warn that you will give a time-out if a rule is broken.
4. Pick a place for time-out.
5. Pick a length of time. A minute or two is enough.
6. If behavior continues, give the time-out. If your child refuses, give a choice of a greater consequence later.
7. Announce the end of time-out.
8. Praise as soon as your child does another behavior you like or refrains from the intolerable behavior.

THE TRIAL RUN:

1. Pick an inexpensive restaurant.
2. Remind the children of the rules.
3. Warn that if the rules are broken, you will all leave the restaurant immediately.
4. Go to the restaurant and order.
5. Praise behaviors you like.
6. When a child breaks a rule, calmly announce you are all leaving.

7. Ignore their protests, graciously accept apologies, and
    tell the children they will have another chance some
    day to try again.

You will not have to do this more than once. Your rules and
warnings will take on greater meaning!

Wrap-up

You have all the tools you need to increase your child's cooperation and reduce conflict in your home. The challenge is in using them: finding things to praise, having the patience to ignore, remaining calm and firm in your limit setting. And doing all these consistently! Use the Trouble Shooting Guide on the next page to help you remember to apply what you have learned.

Following the trouble shooting you will find twenty Battle Plans to help you with specific troublesome behaviors. Rely on the Battle Plans for emergency moments. Tear out the Whining plan and carry it with you in your pocket or purse. Tack the Fighting battle plan inside a kitchen cupboard door for easy reach. Keep the Interrupting battle plan near the telephone, of course!

Parenting is an ongoing challenge. Each new age and stage brings both delightful and annoying behaviors. You can use the *Win the Whining War* tools to increase the new behaviors you like and make the annoying ones manageable. If you find chaos starting to reign, you may be forgetting to praise, giving in to whining and tantrums, lecturing and nagging again, and not following through on your threats (warnings). That's the time to re-read a bit and use the tools.

You can have relief. You can win the whining war and all the other skirmishes. You may even survive long enough to coach your own child in his or her parenting!

Trouble Shooting Guide

Use these steps to improve any problem situation.

1. Look at the situation. Identify the behaviors you like, dislike, and find intolerable.

2. Praise what you like.

3. Ignore what you dislike while you wait for a behavior you can praise.

4. To get your child to start a behavior:
   Give an invitation to cooperate—
   a choice, announcement, or when/then deal.

5. Introduce a Better Behavior Chart.
   a. Select behaviors (easy and challenging ones) and rewards.
   b. Observe your child with private records.
   c. Go public with the chart.
   d. Praise and reward immediately, ignore non-compliance.

6. To get your child to stop a behavior:
   Give a command.

7. If she doesn't stop:
   Give a warning of a consequence.

8 If she doesn't stop then:
Follow through with the consequence.

9. Be consistent. Everytime she repeats the behavior, give the consequence.

10. Use the family meeting:
    a. Define the problem and think of possible solutions.
    b. Set a meeting.
    c. Maintaining a calm tone, state the problem clearly, and ask for ideas.
    d. Come to an agreement through compromise or negotiation.
    e. Assess the situation in a follow-up meeting.

11. PRAISE your child's success.

Battle Plans

In times of heated confrontation, use the following Battle Plans. These are concise strategies which use all the tools presented in *Win the Whining War & Other Skirmishes* plus extra helpful hints. For any other behavior which concerns you, apply the framework presented in the Trouble Shooting Guide. In order to use these Battle Plans successfully, you must have read the entire book.

On the following pages find Battle Plans for:
arguing
bad language
biting
car trouble
complaining
dawdling
fighting
interrupting
lying
nail biting
name-calling/teasing
rudeness
sloppiness
spitting
sulking
talking back
tantrums
tantrums in public
tattling
whining

Arguing

Is this a behavior I like, dislike or find intolerable?
   Dislike

What should I do?
   Ignore child's arguing.
   Praise child's doing what you have asked.

STRATEGY

1.   Ignore the arguing. It takes two to battle. Don't engage.

2.   Praise compliance (even if your child grumbles). When he starts to comply, say "thank you."

3.   Try the broken record technique. Repeat the command until you get compliance, then praise.
Dad: It's time to feed your dog.
Child: Why should I?
Dad: It's time to feed your dog.
Child: It's not my dog.
Dad: It's time to feed your dog.
Child: Stop saying that. [HINT: a sure sign child is weakening!]
Dad: It's time to feed your dog.
Child: All right!
Dad: Thank you.

4.   If your child continues to argue with your request, give a warning of a consequence.

Remember that kids comply with chores reluctantly. They are not going to say, "Yes, mother dear" with big smiles on their faces. The best you may get is stomping off to do what you asked, mumbling hateful things just out of earshot. That's when you must be ready to acknowledge the effort with a simple, "Thank you."

Bad Language

Is this a behavior I like, dislike or find intolerable?
  Dislike (almost intolerable)

What should I do?
  Ignore child's bad language.
  Praise child's using acceptable words to express anger.

STRATEGY

1. Ignore (YES!) She's doing it to get your reaction, so stop reacting!!!

2. Give positive attention to words you like.
    In the same conversation a child may use language you dislike and acceptable words. Be sure to attend positively to the words you like. This will feel strange: turning to your child one second and turning calmly away the next. That's okay. When you ignore you give the message to the child that "bad words aren't heard." He may just as well not waste his breath.

3. Allow nonsense words. "Greeblepuss." "Bullbunion." "Nastermuck." Give prizes to the most creative "swearwords." Adds a little humor, dissipates anger, gives fun alternative to cursing.

4. Announce you're going to ignore the bad language. Then ignore until the experimenting stops. All children use bathroom language and try out bad words. Ignoring is very effective when used at the time they are first experimenting.
Melinda: Winnie the Poo-Poo is a pee-pee.
Grandmother: Those are very silly words, Melinda, and my ears don't
          hear them.

5. Don't take her swearing personally. An older child may use bad language out of habit, picked up from friends. If you overreact, the cursing will increase. Give a little friendly-sounding reminder: "Susie, I'd rather not hear that in the house." She may surprise you by simply saying, "Okay, Mom."

6. Say the bad word yourself. What fun are bad words if your parents use them?
Rob: [drops a stack of papers] Shit!
Dad: Rob, I'm not fond of the word shit. Don't use it when I'm here."

7. If the amount of bad language becomes intolerable, give a consequence: fine the child twenty-five or fifty cents per word (of course,

the same standard must apply to all members of the household who use such language).

8. Watch your language! Children follow your model.

Biting

Is this a behavior I like, dislike or find intolerable?
> Intolerable (biting another child)
> Dislike (toddler biting me)

What should I do?
> Set a limit when child bites another child (or older child bites anyone).
> Ignore little child's biting me.
> Praise child's using words to express anger, coming for help, playing
> well with other child.

STRATEGY

1.   Give a command. Keep it simple, clear and short: "You may not bite."
For a very little child of two or three, the first experiments in biting may be
stopped by giving a strong command of "No biting." Once the rule is
established you may have a standing warning that "If you bite, I'll take
your friend home."

2.   If the biting stops, give praise.
> "You and Josh are playing very nicely now, thank you."
> "I like the way you boys are sharing the truck. That's great."

3.   If he bites again, give a warning of time-out.
> "If you bite one more time, you will have a time-out."

4.   If he doesn't stop, give a time-out. (one minute per year of child)
> "You bit Josh. Go to the time-out chair for three minutes."

5.   When time-out is over, don't lecture.
> "Your time-out is over. You may play with Josh now."

6.   Every time he bites, give a time-out (slightly longer each time).

7.   You may give a consequence instead of time-out, such as:
> If he bites a sibling, he must play alone for fifteen minutes.
> If he bites, he goes to bed fifteen minutes early.

8.   If you possibly can, ignore when your toddler bites you. The "ouch"
you screech is great fun for your child. Looking angry is a payoff, too.
Give no reaction.

9.   Don't bite back! That teaches your child that it's okay to bite if you're
big.

Car Trouble: squabbling, seatbelt refusal, screaming, etc.

Is this a behavior I like, dislike or find intolerable?
Dislike (verging on the intolerable)

What should I do?
Ignore child's complaining, minor squabbling, arguing.
When/then deal with seatbelt refusal, poking, hitting, kicking, screaming.
Praise child's riding in car quietly, engaging in conversation, playing word games etc.

STRATEGY

1. Ignore the complaints, don't listen to the squabbling.

2. Praise behavior you like.

3. Use the when/then deal. Simply bring the car to the side of the road and turn off the engine. Remain silent. Read a magazine, a road map, your address book. Look for birds. Watch for animal shapes in the clouds. Soon your child will say, "Drive, dad." You say, "When you are quiet (your belt is fastened, you keep your hands to yourself), then we will drive." After a minute of silence or cooperation say, "Thank you. We can go now." and start the car. Repeat the stopping as often as you need. It is very effective in letting children know you mean business.

4. Don't ignore silence, cooperation or compliance. Don't just savor the quiet moment. Be sure to tell your child how much you appreciate her cooperating in the car.

5. For legitimate complaints, empathize by mirroring feelings:
Child: It's taking forever to get there.
Dad: Yes, It is a very long drive. Thanks for being so patient.

Complaining

Is this a behavior I like, dislike or find intolerable?
   Dislike

What should I do?
   Ignore child's whiny, nagging complaining.
   Praise child's expressing legitimate complaints in a non-whiny voice.

Note: It's not so much what a child complains about as how he complains. Sure, we want her to be able to directly express feelings, but in a way that isn't irritating.
We don't want: "Yuk, that green stuff is gross! Get it off my plate."
We'd prefer: "Just a little of the green stuff, please."

STRATEGY

1.   Praise your child's politeness, patience and understanding.
   "Thank you for not complaining about the lima beans at Grandma's. I know you don't like them. Just leaving them on your plate was fine."

2.   Give empathy to non-whiny direct, expression of feelings .
Child: It's so hot in here, Mom.
Mom: Yes it is, it's very warm. Let me help you roll up your sleeves.

3.   Announce you are going to ignore complaining. Tell your child what you want instead. "My ears don't work for complaining. If you have a problem, tell me in a normal voice."

4.   Don't give in or the complaints will continue! Ignore the complaining and it will stop.

5.   Listen to yourself. Do you complain? Are you teaching your child by your example? If you are, catch yourself. Model the behavior you want from your child.

Dawdling

Is this a behavior I like, dislike or find intolerable?
    Dislike

What should I do?
    Ignore child's dawdling, daydreaming, getting distracted, being "lazy".
    Praise child's sticking to task, following through, finishing.

STRATEGY

1.   Ignore. (Yes, I do mean ignore! What good is nagging doing!) You need infinite patience to ignore this one. Dawdling seems to be a several year stage for many boys and girls. Don't show your exasperation or the dawdling will become worse.

2.   Praise attempts at sticking to a task, finishing, following through. (Okay, so exaggerate a little.)
    "Good job finishing your homework."
    "Boy, that was quick setting the table."
    "You got dressed fast as lighting."

3.   Avoid labeling and name-calling. Your child will accept the label "lazy" or "slowpoke" and decide that is true about himself.

4.   Make a Better Behavior Chart (BBC) for the most problematic time period of the day. Include on the chart the tasks and the time you want them completed. Be sure to include some behaviors your child readily does and take private records to ensure success. Give lots of praise when your child completes behaviors on time.

5.   Make a game out of it. Time him. See if he can "do it faster than yesterday." Challenge him to set an "all time record." Then praise him for his speed.

6.   Use upbeat music. My kids put on their favorite music tape for room cleaning. Soon they are dancing and singing and working rapidly.

7.   Let your child surprise you. Most kids love to surprise their parents. You can have an older sibling plant the idea. ("Hey, let's surprise mom. Get dressed really quickly and hide under the covers. When she comes in, boy, will she be surprised!") The only problem with this game is that your child will want to do it every morning and if you happen to see him before he has surprised you, he will be very disappointed. For kids five and under you can say, "I'll go back to the kitchen and forget. You can still surprise me."

Fighting

Is this a behavior I like, dislike or find intolerable?
  Dislike (bickering, bothering, pre-fighting)
  Intolerable (hitting, fighting)

What should I do?
  Ignore child's pre-fighting.
  Praise child's playing together well, solving own problems.
  Set limits on child's hitting.

STRATEGY

1.   Ignore minor teasing, bickering, name-calling, if the children are close in age, size, or power. Give kids opportunity to handle problems themselves. Tell them, "You guys work it out."

2.   Praise moments of getting along, playing well. When it's quiet, seek them out. Catch them being good and give loads of attention for it. Give rewards: it's well worth it to you. Don't ever ignore children when they are playing well.

3.   Give them a choice: do you want to play together or separately? Give each twenty minutes of play time in separate areas of the home/yard. Soon they will tire of the independent play and brother or sister will seem much more interesting.

LIMIT SETTING STRATEGY

1.   Give a command. Keep it simple.
   "You may not fight. You must keep your hands to yourself."

2.   If the hitting stops, give praise.
   "You're doing a great job keeping your hands to yourself."

3.   If he hits, give a warning of a consequence or a time-out.
   "If you hit again, you may not play with your brother (sister) for
      twenty minutes."
   "If you hit again, you will have a ten minute time-out."
   "Stop fighting now, you two, or you will both lose ten minutes of TV
      time tonight."

4.   If he doesn't stop, give the consequence or time-out.
   "You hit your brother. You may not play with him for twenty minutes.
Charlie gets to choose where he wants to play, outside or in the bedroom.
You will play in the other." Or "You hit your brother. Go to the time-out

chair. I'm setting the timer for ten minutes." Or "That's it, boys, for fighting you lose ten minutes of TV time."

5.   When consequence/time-out is over, don't lecture. Simply announce "You two may play together now" or "Your time-out is over."

6.   Every time hitting occurs, give the consequence, lengthening the time by one or two minutes.

7.   After the above sequence has occurred once, give a standing warning that any time your child hits his sibling, he will earn a consequence. "You know we do not allow hitting. Every time you hit your brother you will get a time-out."

8.   After a consequence for hitting has been earned and paid, listen well for cooperation. If they play well for three minutes, if you hear any words of cooperation, praise them immediately. I sometimes hand out nickels or dimes to my two children when I catch them being good. The surprise reward and my praise give extra incentive.

Interrupting

Is this a behavior I like, dislike or find intolerable?
 Dislike

What should I do?
 Ignore child's interrupting.
 Praise child's using "excuse me" (stage one) and
  letting you talk with others without interruptions (stage two).

STRATEGY - STAGE ONE

1.   Announce you're going to ignore interruptions and do so. Focus on your conversation. Turn your body, eyes, attention away from your child. Give all of your attention to the other person. Don't allow child's increasing volume to divert you.

2.   Teach her to say "excuse me please" and only allow her to interrupt you with an "excuse me."

3.   Give her your attention when she says, "Excuse me."
 "Yes, Maddie, what would you like?"

STRATEGY - STAGE TWO

1.   Tell her not to interrupt you for a certain period of time. (Start with two minutes and increase to fifteen).
 "I will be on the telephone for ten minutes. I am setting the timer. You may interrupt me if it is an emergency. I'll let you know when I am off the phone."

2.   After the time is up, go to your child and praise him.
 "Thank you for not interrupting while I was on the phone. That was very helpful."

3.   Model politeness for your child. When your child is playing with another or on the telephone, don't interrupt unless it is important and you say "excuse me" yourself!

4.   Offer an incentive with a when/then deal:
 "Mr. Flores and I will be talking for a while. If you will let us talk without interrupting, then I'll play a game with you."

Lying

Is this a behavior I like, dislike or find intolerable?
    Dislike (occasional) and find intolerable (persistent)

What should I do?
    Praise child's telling the truth.
    Set limit on persistent lying.

STRATEGY - PREVENTION

1.   Look behind the lie. Why do children lie? In most cases, school age children lie to avoid punishment. Coming down hard on your child when he lies will not make him stop lying. It may just inspire deviousness.

2.   Don't interrogate. If you know your child has done something you don't like, don't keep asking, "Did you break the pitcher?" Simply state, "I know you broke the pitcher, now I want help cleaning it up."

3.   If your child insists he "didn't do it" avoid the battle. To save face your child may insist he's innocent in the matter (so much so he may start to believe it). Say something like, "Perhaps you didn't break the pitcher. If I've made a mistake I will apologize to you. Right now, however, get the broom and dustpan."

4.   Praise truthfulness. Most children will—on occasion—tell parents the bad news: "You'll probably be mad, Mom, I spilled my milk." Take that opportunity to praise or reward telling the truth. "Thank you for telling me you spilled. I know you were worried I'd be mad, but I appreciate your being honest." If you do this when a child is young, she will be less likely to lie; after all, her parent can handle the truth.

5.   Remember: the fantasies of the pre-schooler are wishes more than lies. Respond to a fantasy wish by saying, "You sure would like that to be able to happen."

6.   Teach the importance of truth. The fairy tales *Pinocchio* and *The Boy Who Cried Wolf* give a vivid picture of the consequences of lying.

7.   Model honesty. Admit your own mistakes. Go easy on exaggeration. Don't lie in front of your child or have your child lie for you. (If the phone rings and you don't want to talk to anyone, don't have your child say, "She's not home.")

8.   Praise all your child's desirable behaviors; lying can be an attention seeking device. Re-read Step Two of the book to make sure you are giving

your child plenty of terrific ways to get attention.

9.   Make a Better Behavior Chart which includes lots of behaviors your child is doing well and "tells the truth today."

10. Set a limit on lying with a command, warning and consequence (loss of TV time or time-out). Don't lecture. Remain calm. Repeat as necessary.

Nail biting

Is this a behavior I like, dislike or find intolerable?
   Dislike

What should I do?
   Ignore child's biting nails.
   Praise child's keeping hands from mouth.

STRATEGY

1.   Ignore the nail biting. Nagging at your child will only increase this habit, which may be a sign of anxiety.

2.   Praise efforts at not biting, keeping hands away from mouth, resting in lap, folded, etc.

3.   Keep nails short. Much nail biting occurs as an attempt at clipping, evening off.

4.   Ask your child if he would like help stopping nail biting. Offer to give a non-verbal reminder, such as a hand signal, when you see him bite his nails. Your child may not be aware when he is biting and a friendly (not critical) reminder could help. Be sure to praise him for stopping; watch for a few minutes and praise again if he keeps his hands from his mouth.

5.   Encourage an activity that keeps hands busy during TV time or whenever your child tends to bite his nails, such as twiddling his thumbs, clenching fists, drawing or doodling, crocheting, shuffling a deck of cards, playing with beads.

6.   Make a Better Behavior Chart. Select a daily period of child when you have observed nail biting occurring. Break down that time period into small segments. Praise and reward your child with a sticker or star on the chart for "keeping hands from face." Remember to ignore failure, remind in a neutral way, and praise success. As your child increases the time he is able not to nail bite, you may use longer time segments.

Name-calling/Teasing

Is this a behavior I like, dislike or find intolerable?
> Dislike (calling me names, using silly names, kids calling each other names)
>
> Intolerable (cruel, hurtful words or racial slurs, older child taunting younger child)

What I should do?
> Ignore child's silly name-calling/teasing.
> Set limit on child's cruel name-calling/teasing.
> Praise using acceptable words to express anger with another.

STRATEGY

1.   Ignore the name-calling or teasing.
     If your child calls you a name, don't give any attention. The thrill will soon be gone.

2.   Teach ignoring to your child and playmates by reciting:
     "Sticks and stones may break my bones, but names will never hurt me."

3.   Wait for and praise (give attention to) using words to express anger.

LIMIT SETTING STRATEGY

1.   Give a command. Keep it simple.
     "I do not allow name-calling."
     "You may not tease."
     "No name-calling."

2.   If the name-calling or teasing stops, give praise.
     "I did not hear any more name-calling. I appreciate that."

3.   If he name-calls or teases again, give a warning.
     "If I hear one more name called, you will have a time out."

4.   If he doesn't stop, give a time-out.
     "That's name-calling. Go to the time out chair for eight minutes (eight year-old child)."

5.   When time-out is over, don't lecture. (See Family Meeting below)
     Dismiss child from chair with "Thank you for taking time-out."

6.   Every time name-calling or teasing occurs, give a time-out, lengthening it by one minute each time.

7.   You may give a consequence instead of time-out, such as:
     If playing outside, child must come in from play for a fifteen minutes. If he called names at friend, allow friend to go home. If he called names at his sibling, give sibling privilege of playing alone for half an hour. On any day child calls names, he goes to bed fifteen minutes early. Set a fine: a quarter for every name he calls.

8.   Give a standing warning. After the above sequence has occurred once, tell him that any time you hear name-calling or teasing there will be an automatic consequence.
     "You know we do not allow name-calling. Every time you call a name at your brother you will get a time-out."

Rudeness

Is this a behavior I like, dislike or find intolerable?
> Dislike (rude remarks, interrupting, being impolite, not saying please and thank you, reaching across the table)

What should I do?
> Ignore rude remarks.
> Praise politeness.
> Set limits on rudeness which becomes mean or hurtful.

STRATEGY

1.   Praise politeness and good manners. If a child says, "please" or "thank you" or "excuse me" give positive attention to it.

2.   Ignore rude requests. Don't pass the butter to someone who says "gimme the butter." Keep on talking (ignore) when child interrupts conversation.

3.   Model good manners. Be courteous. Don't interrupt. Start early on treating your child courteously, and your child will follow your example.

4.   Be specific and clear about what you expect from your child.
"Answer the telephone with "Hello, this is____, who's calling please?"

5.   Use clear commands to set limits:
"Don't reach across the table for the salt."
"If you need to interrupt, please say 'excuse me'."

6.   Be realistic. Your child will need a reminder or two.

7.   Follow up with praise when you see your child behaving well.

8.   Find out how he behaves at friends' homes. You may be pleasantly surprised by reports of excellent manners. Most kids do a better job when parents are not around. Be sure to tell him about good reports and how proud you are.

9.   If the rudeness to you becomes cruel, dig in your heals and ignore.

10. If the rudeness to another child becomes cruel, use the limit setting strategy from the Battle Plan for Name-calling.

Sloppiness

Is this a behavior I like, dislike or find intolerable?
 Dislike (leaving clothes and toys around the house)
 Intolerable (I can only stand it for so long)

What I should do?
 Ignore dawdling, complaints, minimum efforts, etc.
 Praise any attempt at picking up, putting things away.
 Set limits if situation becomes intolerable.

STRATEGY

1.   Praise every effort, however small. "Great job putting your clothes in the hamper this morning." "Thank you for straightening your bed." "You're keeping your room pretty neat this week, that's terrific."

2.   Don't nag. I won't go so far as to say that being sloppy will be cured by ignoring it, but I do know that nagging is worthless at making a child neat.

3.   Break room-cleaning into small, manageable tasks. (See Chapter 7) Praise the small efforts. One parent rewards each task by allowing the children to watch one cartoon from a collection she has videotaped. When the cartoon is over the next task is assigned.

4.   The when/then deal is one of two ways my children will gleefully straighten their room. The best job was the day I announced, "If you kids have cleaned your room—including your closet—by 11:00, this afternoon we will go get the new kitten." I'm not suggesting you get a new kitten every day, but it was the quickest, cleanest job the two ever did straightening their room.

5.   The when/then deal can be used in this way:
Child: May I go out and play?
Parent: When you have picked up your toys, then you may go out.

6.   Make a Better Behavior Chart. The chart items might be:
 makes bed before school
 puts clothes in the hamper morning and evening
 leaves floor toy-free
 straightens desk and bureau top
 hangs up coat and backpack

4.   Use a warning of a consequence if all else fails.

5.   Model neatness. Your child will tend to do as you do.

Spitting

Is this a behavior I like, dislike or find intolerable?
    Intolerable

What I should do?
    Set limits on spitting.

STRATEGY

1.   Spitting is a behavior that is more disgusting than harmful, but most find it intolerable, therefore you want to set a limit on it.

2.   Give a command. Keep it simple.
    "Spitting is not allowed."
    For a very little child, of two or three, the first experiments in spitting will likely be stopped by giving a strong command of "No spitting."

3.   If the spitting stops, give praise.
    "Thank you for not spitting."

4.   If she spits again, give a warning.
    "If you spit one more time, you will have a time out."

5.   If she doesn't stop, give a time-out.
    "You spit again. Go to the time out chair for five minutes."
    When time-out is over, don't lecture.
    "Thank you for taking time-out."
    Every time spitting occurs lengthening time-out by one minute.

6.   You may give a consequence instead of time-out, such as:
    If playing outside, child must come in from play for fifteen minutes.
    If she spits at friend, send the friend home.
    If she spits at sibling, give sibling privilege of playing alone or in
        another room for a half-hour.
    On any day child spits, she goes to bed fifteen minutes early.

7.   Give a standing warning. Give consequence any time child spits.
    "You know we do not allow spitting. Anytime you spit you will get a time-out (or a consequence)."

Sulking

Is this a behavior I like, dislike or find intolerable?
Dislike

What I should do:
Ignore child's sulking.
Praise child's coming to you to talk about feelings.

Although sulking is quiet, it can be very irritating when your child hangs about, draped on furniture, lower lip nearly dragging on the floor, clearly unhappy but unwilling to talk about the problem. You feel helpless.

STRATEGY

1.   Announce you are going to ignore the moping. Tell her that you would be glad to speak with her if she wants, but that you'll leave her alone until she wants to talk to you.

2.   Give positive attention (listen to her troubles) when she stops sulking and talks about what is bothering her.

3.   Let her know that putting feelings into words might help. Tell her she can talk to you, talk to someone else, write in a diary, write a letter, or write a story about a girl with a problem like hers. Tell her you know she will feel better once she sorts through her feelings.

4.   Give empathy (support her feelings) rather than advice.
Listen to her feelings and let you know you understand (if you do). Offer advice only if she wants it. If you are a good listener, she will soon learn it is safe to come to you for help. She'll stop sulking too.

5.   Although it is normal for girls and boys to sulk (an indirect asking for help), watch for signs of depression: marked increase or decrease in eating or sleeping habits, loss or gain of weight, lack of energy, disinterest in activities, and school failure. These are signs which should not be ignored; you should consult a physician and a mental health professional about your child.

Talking Back

Is this a behavior I like, dislike or find intolerable?
    Dislike

What should I do?
    Ignore child's talking back.
    Praise child's doing what you have asked.

STRATEGY

1.   Ignore the back talk.
Mom: It's time to feed your dog.
Child: Why should I?
Mom: [turns to stove] There's more dog food in the back cupboard if you need it.

2.   Wait for and praise (give attention to) compliance.
Mom: It's time to feed your dog.
Child: [gives loud sigh, but walks toward kitchen] It's not my dog.
Mom: [ignoring sighs and back talk] Thank you, Silvia.

3.   Announce you are ignoring the back talk.
    "Silvia, I'm not going to listen to your back talk. I expect you to feed your dog now."

4.   Give a warning of a consequence. Let's say you allow your child one-half hour of TV time each school night. You have told your child to empty the trash (it's overflowing and the trash is his job):
Dad: Frank, empty the trash, please.
Frank: Why should I?
Dad: That's back talk, Frank. I asked you to empty the trash.
Frank: Why can't you do it?
Dad: You will lose five minutes of TV time tonight if you keep it up.
Frank: Keep what up?
Dad: That's five minutes.
Frank: Right. Thanks a lot.
Dad: That's ten minutes. Empty the trash now, please.
Frank: That's not fair. Nobody else has jobs around here.
Dad: That's fifteen.
Frank: Okay, okay. I'll empty the damn trash. [stomps off]
Dad: Thank you, Frank. [ignores stomping—Frank's face-saving device]

5.   If your child has a complaint, have him comply with the request before you discuss it. Say something like, "When you've emptied the trash, we can talk about your problem with it."

Remember: at about age five, all children talk back to their parents: "Who says?" "Why should I?" "Why don't you?" "Who cares?" and so forth. By ignoring completely, you remove the payoff (your anger and punishment). Soon you'll hear less and less back talk. Ignoring works with talking back because the purpose is get your reaction. Stop reacting and there'll be no reason to continue the back talk.

Tantrums

Is this a behavior I like, dislike or find intolerable?
Dislike

What should I do?
Ignore child's tantrums (angry screaming, kicking, etc.).
Praise child's using his words to express feelings.

STRATEGY

1. Ignore the tantrum. Focus on something else.

2. Announce you're going to ignore the tantrum.
Parent: [quietly near his ear] Sam, I will not listen to you while you're kicking. When you stop, we can talk."

3. Praise (give attention to) using words to express anger.
Child: [stops kicking and screaming] I hate you. You're a bad mommy.
Parent: You're very mad at Mommy. You wanted the scissors and Mommy said no.
Child: Yes [with big pout]. I want the scissors.
Parent: I'm glad you used your words to tell me. I understand how mad you are. I will help you cut, but you may not use the scissors by yourself.

4. Give yourself a pep talk:
"I can outlast him. He's a child. I'm the parent."

5. Calmly leave the room. Stay away until he quiets.

6. If your very little child bangs his head on the floor when angry, calmly put a pillow or your hand under his head. Remain as relaxed as possible as you try to ignore the tantrum.

7. If your older child is still throwing tantrums it may be because you gave in to them when he was younger. Have a family meeting. Let him know what he may do when he is angry (tell the person, punch a pillow, etc.), but tell him you will not listen to him until he uses words to express himself. When he is ready to talk, you will be happy to listen.

Remember: nearly all children two to four have some tantrums. To keep them to a minimum, ignore consistently. By giving attention to him when he uses his words (instead of screams) your child's tantrums will decrease. By age five your child should be able to express his feelings verbally.

Tantrums in Public

Is this a behavior I like, dislike or find intolerable?
    Dislike (tantrum with me)
    Intolerable (if disturbing others)

What should I do?
    Ignore child's tantrum with me.
    Praise child's using words to express anger, cooperating in public.
    Set a limit when child's tantrums disturb others.

STRATEGY

1.   Announce firmly (with eye contact) that you will ignore the tantrum.
    "I will not listen to this noise you are making. I'll be reading a magazine right over there."

2.   Ignore the tantrum. Keep your child in your sight while you focus your attention on something else. Ignore by engaging with adults around you. Smile at people. Say, "Isn't parenting fun?" Make small talk. Breathe deeply. Continue to focus on anything else but your child until he makes an attempt to calm himself and use words to express his feelings. Then praise.

3.   If he does not calm down, give a warning of a consequence. Wait a moment to give your child a chance to exert self-control. Praise any attempt to calm himself and use words.
Parent: Keep your feet to yourself and use your words or we will have to
         leave.
Child: [Stops tantrum, whines but uses words] But I want the cookies.
Parent: Thank you for using your words. I understand you want a cookie.
         You'll have a cookie tonight for dessert.

4.   Follow through with consequence or time-out.
    a.   Warning: If you do not stop kicking and screaming, we will leave.
    b.   Wait a short time for your child to save face and comply.
    c.   Follow through with consequence if the tantrum continues.
          Say firmly, "You are still kicking. We have to leave now." Calmly,
          walk to the door of the room or building. Don't make eye contact.
          Make every attempt to conceal your anger. Wait where he can see
          you, pretending to be interested in something. He may follow you,
          but at a distance to save face. When he's near, say, "Thank you"
          and leave the building. Take him home. Do not lecture. Only give
          attention to behaviors you like.

5.   If he doesn't follow you and is small, carry your child to another room, restroom, a hallway, outside or to the car. He may kick and scream. Be

firm, but neutral. Give a time-out.

6.   If your older child will not leave, give her a choice:
Parent: You either come with me now quietly or go to bed fifteen minutes
          early. Which do you choose?

Remember: Once you can set limits at home, you'll be able to set limits in public. Just have a plan in mind before you go and follow though on giving consequences. Don't worry so much about people around you. See page 157 for how to do a trial run.

Tattling

Is this a behavior I like, dislike or find intolerable?
  Dislike

What should I do?
  Ignore child's tattling.
  Praise child's solving her own problems with others and minding her
    own business.

STRATEGY

1. Ignore the tattling. A simple way to let a child know you are not interested in tattling is to give a simple "uh-huh" or a "thank you" but then turn your attention to something else.

2. Praise solving own problems. When you observe children working problems out, give plenty of praise.

3. It's better to tattle than to hit back. If your child tends to strike out when feeling provoked, give permission to her to ask for your help in solving the problem with the other child.

4. Cross-complaining or two-way tattling (two kids running to you to referee) can be reduced by a simple prompt: "You two need to work it out." If it's a heated exchange, give them a choice: "Since you're both feeling angry, would you rather play separately or together?" Given this option, they may well decide to continue playing together.

Whining

Is this a behavior I like, dislike or find intolerable?
Dislike

What should I do?
Ignore child's whining.
Praise child's using a normal voice.

STRATEGY

1.   Ignore the whining. (Focus on something else.)
Focus on the second hand of your watch or a clock. Give yourself a mental exercise. Try to remember the multiplication tables.

2.   Wait for and praise her using a normal voice.
Parent: I like the voice you're using. You sound very grown up.

3.   Announce you're going to ignore the whining.
"I am not going to listen to whining. When you use your normal voice I will answer you."

4.   Use a little prompt as a reminder.
"That's funny, my ears aren't working!"

5.   Praise the smallest step in the right direction, any attempt at using a normal voice.
"Thank you, Melinda, I hear you trying very hard to use your big girl voice."

6.   Check out every adult in the household. Who's rewarding the whining by giving in or showing frustration? Work together. Ignore!

7.   Make a Better Behavior Chart. Chart items may be in time increments or tied to specific tasks. Use private records to ensure success. Be sure to praise any attempt at using a normal voice. You don't have to cover the whole day with chart items. I find that focusing on one part of the day and rewarding the successes creates a positive atmosphere and increases good behavior throughout the day.

8.   Listen to yourself. Do you get a little whiny now and then? Your child may be following your example.

Remember: Many children go through a whining stage at age three. If you ignore consistently, and praise talking in a normal voice your child will stop whining. Don't give in!

A Final Word

If you came from a home in which you were not praised it may be very hard for you to remember to praise your child. Your parents may have thought it unnecessary to praise you, that your good behavior was expected and chores and homework were to be done without question. You may think, "Well I turned out okay, so why do I have to praise my child?"

You may have indeed turned out fine, but remember how it felt to be a child. Would you have liked more positive attention, more encouragement, more interest shown in your schoolwork or your ideas and feelings? Would it have felt good for your parents to thank you when you helped or cooperated, succeeded at something or just did the best you could?

Not only does responding to your children with positive attention give you a way to guide behavior, but it helps them as well. We hear a lot about self-esteem and recognize its importance in a child becoming a healthy, mature adult. An upbringing with praise, encouragement and recognition from parents helps a child know it's okay to love and like oneself, okay to hold oneself in high esteem.

If you find yourself unable to give these kinds of positive messages to your child or that your tolerance for noise and tantrums is so low, that in spite of your best efforts you find yourself still screaming or spanking, consider getting professional help from a social worker (LCSW), psychologist (PhD), psychiatrist (MD), or marriage, family, child counselor (MFCC).

But if you are able to apply the tools suggested in *Win the Whining & Other Skirmishes* and your child's behavior does not change, you may want to have your child evaluated by a child psychiatrist or psychologist.

Index

Order Form

_____ Win the Whining War & Other Skirmishes - $12.95

_____ Childcare Southern California - $9.95
The only complete guide to finding child care in Los Angeles, Orange, and Ventura counties. Includes articles for parents on all aspects of the child care search and listings for all the more than 3,000 day care centers, preschools and school-age extended day programs licensed by the state in those three counties.

Please add $2.50 shipping for first book, .50 for each additional book. Michigan residents add sales tax.

Name: _____

Address:_____

_____
    City   *State*   *Zip*

Phone: (_____)_____   Total Enclosed: $_____

Send to: Publishers Distribution Service
121 E. Front Street, Suite 203
Traverse City, MI 49684

or

ORDER TOLL FREE 1-800-345-0096